LITERACY
COACHING

DALE E. MOXLEY
ROSEMARYE T. TAYLOR

LITERACY COACHING

A HANDBOOK
for
SCHOOL LEADERS

A Joint Publication

National Association of Secondary School **PRINCIPALS**

CORWIN PRESS

CORWIN PRESS
A SAGE Publications Company
Thousand Oaks, California

For information:

Corwin Press
A Sage Publications Company
2455 Teller Road
Thousand Oaks, California 91320
www.corwinpress.com

Sage Publications Ltd.
1 Oliver's Yard
55 City Road
London EC1Y 1SP
United Kingdom

Sage Publications India Pvt. Ltd.
B-42, Panchsheel Enclave
Post Box 4109
New Delhi 110 017 India

Printed in the United States of America.

Library of Congress Cataloging-in-Publication Data

Moxley, Dale E.
Literacy coaching : a handbook for school leaders / Dale E. Moxley,
Rosemarye T. Taylor.
    p. cm.
Includes bibliographical references and index.
ISBN 1-4129-2632-7 (cloth) — ISBN 1-4129-2633-5 (pbk.))
    1. Language arts (Elementary)—United States. 2. Language arts (Secondary)—United States. 3. Literacy programs—United States—Handbooks, manuals, etc. I. Taylor, Rosemarye, 1950- II. Title.
LB1576.M823 2006
428.4'071—dc22

                                                              2005026853

This book is printed on acid-free paper.

06   07   08   09   10   9   8   7   6   5   4   3   2

Acquisitions Editor:	Elizabeth Brenkus
Editorial Assistant:	Desirée Enayati
Production Editor:	Jenn Reese
Copy Editor:	Heather Moore
Typesetter:	C&M Digitals (P) Ltd.
Proofreader:	Dennis Webb
Indexer:	Ellen Slavitz
Cover Designer:	Michael Dubowe
Graphic Designer:	Lisa Miller

Contents

Preface

*L*iteracy Coaching is intended to be a practical guide to support development of literacy coach positions, planning for implementation, and follow-up to monitor effectiveness. Initially, the text develops the authors' view of fail-safe literacy systems and provides a context for the examples and recommendations that follow. Teacher-leaders, school and district administrators, and literacy coaches will find much value in the text.

Although there is a research base for fail-safe literacy, literacy coaches are a fairly new position being implemented on a large, national level. In advance of the national movement, the authors developed and implemented the K–12 literacy coach concept and have worked with literacy coaches for several years. Through this experience, they have learned firsthand what yields and hinders success for literacy coaches. The reader will find references to work with literacy coaches in a variety of states in elementary, middle, and high schools as well as district offices.

Acknowledgments

There are literacy coaches in elementary, middle, and high schools and school district levels who should be thanked for striving to make a measurable difference in literacy learning in classrooms every day. In this text, literacy coaches in Florida's Lake County Schools, Seminole County Schools, Sarasota County Schools, and Orange County Public Schools and Logan County Schools, Kentucky, have been used as models for other literacy coaches. These teacher-leaders are pioneers who deserve special recognition for contributing to a new way of thinking about literacy learning and leadership in schools.

In addition to acknowledging these literacy coaches, I particularly want to mention Nancy Fuliehan; we first met when she was a reading resource teacher and I was a middle school principal. Nancy quickly became my literacy coach, just as she was to teachers, helping me grow in literacy learning and leading knowledge and skills. She has continued for more than 30 years as a colleague, friend, mentor, thinker, and model of professionalism on whom other teacher-leaders, literacy coaches, and administrators can rely for reflection and thinking. Thank you, Nancy!

—Rosemarye Taylor

I, too, owe a lot of gratitude to the literacy coaches I have worked with, especially the fantastic group in Lake County. I have learned a great deal from them, and they have been wonderful to work with. The principals have also been receptive to the literacy coach concept, and I am thankful for their support and willingness to work with us. I would also like to thank my colleagues in the curriculum department, Carmen Arnold, Doreathe Cole, Alicia Bermudez, Lisa Gross, Dee Ann Wilson, Claudia Rowe, and Karen Kennen. They are all true literacy leaders. I also owe a great deal to Dr. Rosemarye Taylor. Rose has been a wonderful colleague and friend.

Finally, I thank my best friend and wife, Dr. Susan Moxley, and my daughter, Lea, for their continued support.

—Dale Moxley

PUBLISHER'S ACKNOWLEDGMENTS

Corwin Press gratefully acknowledges the contributions of the following individuals:

John Harrison
Executive Director
NC Middle School Association
Pinehurst, NC

Linda Hargan
Director
Collaborative for Teaching and Learning
Louisville, KY

Marilyn Paull
Principal
Peters Elementary
Garden Grove, CA

Janet Hurt
Associate Superintendent for Curriculum and Instruction
Logan County School District
Russellville, KY

About the Authors

**Dale E. Moxley** is currently Principal at Round Lake Elementary, a Lake County, Florida, charter conversion school. He has an EdD in Educational Leadership and more than 30 years' experience in education and administration. His school level administrative experience includes principal at the elementary, middle, and high school levels, and he has also been the director of secondary curriculum at the district level. His teaching experience ranges from sixth grade through college level and encompasses mathematics, physical education, social studies, and drama. In higher education, he has taught several master's and doctoral level classes in Educational Leadership for the University of Central Florida and National-Louis University.

Dale has received over $2 million in grant funding for education, literacy initiatives, and literacy coaches in the past several years. This grant funding has also included using technology to improve student achievement through literacy enhancement. These grants helped execute the literacy coach concept for the Lake County Schools.

As director of secondary curriculum, Dale helped lead the implementation of the PreK–12 *Just Read, Lake!* reading initiative with Carmen Arnold, director of elementary curriculum. This was a grassroots effort by district staff, local administrators, and school staff to create a fail-safe literacy process across all content areas for PreK–12 students. The literacy process was comprehensive and included professional development; literacy assessment and monitoring; and the roles and responsibilities for administrators, teachers, and literacy coaches. He supervised the literacy coaches for the district and provided for their professional development districtwide during the first three years of the development process.

Dale has also worked with career academies and the small learning community concept. He has made several presentations on this subject, including the Georgia State Tech Prep and National Tech Prep Network conferences. He has also researched how well prepared high school graduates are to enter directly into the workforce.

 **Rosemarye (Rose) T. Taylor,** Associate Professor of Educational Leadership at the University of Central Florida in Orlando, has a rich background including middle and high school teaching and school administration. In addition to serving as a reading, language arts, and Spanish teacher, she also served as a middle and high school administrator and district level administrator in Georgia and Florida. In private sector management, she was the director of professional development for Scholastic, Inc., New York.

Much of her success stems from conceptualizing, creating, and implementing fail-safe systems that work seamlessly to support improvements in student learning. For example, Rose led research, design, and implementation of the Orange County Literacy Program that has successfully impacted thousands of elementary, middle, and high school students and teachers. The classroom concept designed, implemented, and evaluated with her leadership has been produced as a literacy intervention product by Scholastic, Inc. Additionally, in Orange County Public Schools in Orlando, Florida, she designed and implemented a curriculum system including curriculum, instruction, assessment, and professional development, supporting the notion that systems make the work of administrators and teachers easier. These successful systems have a consistent thread. They support the development and implementation of learning communities to advance student achievement by providing structure, which empowers the classroom teachers to make gains day by day.

As Associate Professor of Educational Leadership at the University of Central Florida, her specialty is instructional leadership. Rose has conducted research on leadership particularly as it relates to accountability. Presentations on this topic have been given at University Council of Educational Administration, American Association of Educational Research, American Association of School Administrators, International Reading Association, Association for Supervision and Curriculum Development, McREL's Conference on Leading Learning, National Association of Secondary School Principals, and National Middle School Association conferences. Her articles have been published in *Kappan, Educational Leadership, Middle School Journal, Schools in the Middle, American Secondary Education, AASA Professor, The National Staff Development Journal, Principal Leadership, The School Administrator,* and *International Journal of Education Management.* Three books reflect her commitment to all students learning more through leadership that creates ethical fail-safe systems: *The K–12 Literacy Leadership Fieldbook* (Taylor & Gunter, 2005), *Literacy Leadership for Grades 5–12* (Taylor & Collins, 2003), and *Leading With Character to Improve Student Achievement* (Williams & Taylor 2003). She serves as consultant on literacy, learning communities, curriculum system development, and leadership to schools, districts, and professional organizations.

1 Fail-Safe Literacy Coaching

Most successful people can identify a coach, mentor, or other influential person who challenged them to accomplish more than they had thought possible. The standing joke in administrator meetings is how common the first name Coach is, but the fact is that an effective coach who inspires extraordinary performance from ordinary people is a model of strategic leadership. A successful coach does not offer universal praise or condemnation but instead specific feedback. He is unequivocally clear about the mission and objectives and is, above all, a great teacher who identifies each step that takes the team from vision through execution to success.

(Reeves, 2002, p. 170)

We have found that the literacy coach is the key to positive change in a school or district that has determined that literacy learning is the priority. We worked together—the authors; elementary, middle, and high school faculty; staff; and administration in Lake County Public Schools—from inception of the literacy coach concept, to implementation, monitoring, and evaluation of literacy coaches' impact. The district's literacy plan includes the recommendation of the literacy coach position in each school and is called *Just Read, Lake!* (Lake County Schools, 2003).

Literacy coaches may be school based or district based. They support elementary teachers in day-to-day core reading instruction, teachers who provide literacy intervention, and those who teach other areas. At the middle and high school levels, the literacy coach supports the reading teacher, intervention teachers, and those who teach content curriculum with literacy infusion. Our research and practical application of effectively implementing the literacy coach position to improve student achievement is captured in the chapters that follow.

DEFINING LITERACY

Before we can discuss the concept of literacy coach, we must explain what we mean by literacy. Rose has facilitated the process of defining literacy with many groups of professionals throughout the country representing all grade levels. The definition is always similar and generally incorporates the processes of literacy (reading, writing, speaking, listening, viewing, thinking), but literacy is typically measured as reading and writing. The fail-safe definition of literacy is used for the purpose of this text. *Fail-safe literacy* is defined as listening, viewing, thinking, speaking, reading, writing, and expressing through multiple symbol systems at a developmentally appropriate level.

Most of the literacy processes develop together. Oral language (speaking) develops before print language through viewing, listening, thinking, and multiple symbol systems. Once oral language develops, children begin to make sense of the language patterns and ideally associate oral language with print or make sound-symbol relationships. They begin to understand that words are made of segments or phonemes that when put together have meaning. This is how reading begins. Those who experience improvements in reading and writing know that they develop together, not separately. The term *multiple symbol systems* refers to nonalphabetic communication such as music, art, movement, charts, maps, graphs, mathematical and scientific symbols, and all other communication methods. Multiple symbol systems are included in the fail-safe definition of literacy because we believe that literacy is developed through various experiences; and reading comprehension is measured with charts, maps, and graphs as well as in paragraphs. When the fail-safe literacy definition is used to drive instruction, teachers in elementary, middle, and high schools observe improvements in reading, writing, and content learning.

FAIL-SAFE LITERACY POINT OF VIEW

Although literacy-related instruction has a continually developing research base, we are not going to address the research in detail. We will only provide a brief fail-safe literacy point of view so the reader will have a context for scenarios and examples that appear in the text. As the definition suggests, literacy learning is a synergistic experience that occurs with print. In other words, literacy is thinking with print. To provide students

Table 1.1   Nonnegotiable Expectations of Daily Practice

- Teachers provide phonological awareness instruction for grades K-1 and any other students without mastery.
- Teachers create print and literacy rich K–12 classrooms.
- Teachers read grade-level texts to and with students K–12, both fiction and nonfiction.
- Teachers teach, model, and practice strategies of expert K–12 readers before, during, and after reading.
- Students should have accountable independent reading for a minimum of 20 minutes per day for Grades 1–5 and Grades 6–12, at least for those reading below grade level.

optimal experiences to develop literacy achievement, measured predominately through reading and writing, we support daily instructional expectations on the part of every teacher in a school. It is understood that the nonnegotiable expectations of daily practice are applied in developmentally appropriate ways for students in different grade levels. When present in every classroom every day, the expectations identified in Table 1.1 result in positive changes in student achievement measured as reading, writing, and content learning.

The first four nonnegotiable expectations of daily practice are where teachers provide direct instruction on reading skills; or an environment that supports phonological awareness, fluency, vocabulary development, and comprehension of text; or direct instruction and modeling of strategies. The last nonnegotiable expectation of daily practice, accountable independent reading, is when the students apply what the teachers have taught them by reading a book of their choice on their independent reading level, being held accountable for doing so, and having their growth monitored. It is worth noting that we believe all students should have accountable independent reading for at least 20 minutes per day but acknowledge that it is more difficult to schedule in Grades 7–12, and most students who read on grade level at that point are continuing to read if their school has a culture of literacy.

During the instructional experiences using the nonnegotiable expectations of daily practice, teachers are addressing the elements of reading: phonics, phonemic awareness, vocabulary, fluency, and comprehension (National Institute of Child Health and Human Development, 2000). By ensuring the nonnegotiable expectations of daily practice, teachers will address the elements of reading; each day they strive to improve phonological awareness, vocabulary, fluency, and comprehension of text across all grade levels and in all content areas. These nonnegotiable expectations of daily practice are supported by Wilson and Protheroe

(2004), Protheroe, Shellard, and Turner (2004), and Biancarosa and Snow (2004). These nonnegotiable expectations of daily practice not only are for all teachers, who provide assurance that elementary students learn to read; but they are also for middle and high school students, who have equal access to their content curriculum while learning vocabulary and developing fluency and comprehension of their content texts. These nonnegotiable expectations of daily practice accomplish two important objectives:

1. They improve literacy by addressing the five elements of reading. (See Table 1.2.)

2. They provide access to and comprehension of on-grade-level content texts—thus improving content learning.

If you would like to know more about the fail-safe point of view of literacy, you may want to read *The K–12 Literacy Leadership Fieldbook* (Taylor & Gunter, 2005) and *Literacy Leadership for Grades 5–12* (Taylor & Collins, 2003).

LITERACY COACH

Teachers helping teachers is an informal collaborative approach that has probably been around since the first schools. Recent legislation at the state and national levels, designed to increase student achievement, has brought the *literacy coaching* model to the forefront as a method to assist teachers in improving literacy and learning in all content areas. Coaching support ranges from assisting primary teachers who teach the most basic phonemic awareness to supporting high school teachers with implementation of literacy strategies in all content areas for both struggling and excelling readers. There are questions to be answered before the literacy coach concept can be implemented:

- What is a literacy coach?
- What is literacy coaching?
- How does literacy coaching differ for elementary, middle, and high schools?
- Who is coached and how?
- What are the literacy coach's roles and responsibilities?
- What does the literacy coach need to do before coaching?
- How does the literacy coach ensure effective professional development?
- How can the literacy coach develop relationships with faculty, administrators, staff, and families?
- How will the literacy coach's impact be evaluated?

Table 1.2   Five Reading Elements

Element	Definition	Example
Phonemic Awareness	The ability to hear, identify, and manipulate the individual sounds in spoken words. It is part of phonological awareness.	A child can speak, repeat, and use different words and sounds. He or she learns patterns in speech and repeat those, although sometimes grammatically incorrect, like think, thunk.
Phonics	Understanding the relationship between the letters and the spoken sounds.	A child understands that letters and combinations of letters make specific sounds.
Fluency	Orally reading with appropriate rate, expression, and phrasing.	A child picks up a book and reads it as if in a conversation, with automaticity.
Vocabulary	Words for effective communication when listening, speaking, reading, and writing.	A child knows the words in a passage and the words' meanings without having to struggle.
Comprehension	Understanding the meaning of print.	A child is a fluent reader, knows the vocabulary, and can put in his or her own words what the passage is about.

Based on Taylor, R. T., & Gunter, G. A., p. 18. Used with permission.

Taylor, R. T., & Gunter, G. A. (2005). *The K–12 Literacy Leadership Fieldbook*, p. 18.

We offer time-tested, practical answers to these and other literacy coaching questions to help the reader successfully implement literacy coaching to improve literacy achievement.

REFLECTION

In this chapter, we have provided background knowledge on the fail-safe literacy point of view and an introduction to our literacy coaching perspective. The remaining chapters provide guidance for prospective literacy coaches and those working with literacy coaches on what they need to know and how to acquire the knowledge, skills, and dispositions that will ensure their success. Chapter 2 details the roles and responsibilities of literacy coaches; Chapters 3 and 4 encourage the literacy coach to prepare well before beginning coaching. Building the literacy team and capacity for success is discussed in Chapter 5. Chapter 6 focuses on data study, using data to inform instruction and monitor growth. Because of the critical nature of intensive reading intervention for the neediest students, Chapter 7 is devoted to the literacy coach's role with the associated teachers and students. Professional development is typically the initial focus of literacy coaches, so Chapter 8 provides practical guidance in getting started successfully. Finally, Chapter 9 provides tips for continued success in the role of literacy coach.

TERMS TO REMEMBER

Fail-safe literacy: Systematic literacy learning that ensures success in reading, writing, and content learning; includes the processes of reading, writing, speaking, listening, viewing, and communicating with multiple symbol systems.

Elements of reading: Phonics, phonemic awareness, vocabulary, fluency, comprehension.

Nonnegotiable expectations of daily practice: Daily expectations of all classrooms Grades K–12, core reading, intervention, and content curriculum classes.

2 Literacy Coaching

Working Together and Learning Together

> *People accomplish more together than in isolation; regular, collective dialogue about an agreed-upon focus sustains commitment and feeds purpose; effort thrives on concrete evidence of progress; and teachers learn best from other teacher. We must ensure that these three concepts operate to produce results.*

(Schmoker, 1999, p. 55)

WHAT IS A LITERACY COACH?

Literacy coach and reading coach are sometimes used interchangeably; however, we will be using the term *literacy coach* because reading is developed through the processes of literacy (reading, writing, listening, speaking, viewing, thinking, and communicating through multiple symbol systems). The International Reading Association (IRA) indicates confusion has arisen because the term *literacy coach* is applied to a variety of people and positions such as paraprofessionals or volunteers who read with students (International Reading Association, 2004b). Sturtevant (2003) offered the following definition of literacy coach in *The Literacy Coach: A Key to Improving Teaching and Learning in Secondary Schools*:

Literacy coaches—master teachers who provide essential leadership for the school's entire literacy program. This leadership includes helping to create and supervising a long-term staff development process that supports both the development and implementation of the literacy program over months and years. (p. 11)

Sturtevant notes several other qualities of effective literacy coaches across the nation. In addition to knowledge and skills, the potential coach should have the ability or disposition to establish respect and trust within the school. Literacy coaches often volunteer knowing they will have to spend a substantial amount of time to add reading certification or endorsement to their certificates (p. 13). Clearly, the literacy coach concept is interpreted differently by different people.

The literacy coach takes on many different forms; however, for this text, we will concentrate on the literacy coach as *the teacher-leader who has the responsibility to promote and enhance literacy instruction with the ultimate goal of improving student achievement as measured by reading, writing, and content learning.* The literacy coach is a formal position in the school or district and usually involves some release time from the classroom, which affords time to work with colleagues in a team-building and collaborative manner. Frankly, a literacy coach cannot accomplish all that this text suggests unless the person has the position full time.

There are also inherent differences in the literacy coach position by grade levels served. The elementary literacy coach faces a different scenario each day than the middle or high school literacy coach. The majority of the elementary faculty is teaching reading on a daily basis, and they have had some reading instruction in their professional degree training. So although familiar with reading, the elementary teachers need support with consistent and effective implementation of the core reading program. In contrast, the middle and high school level faculties are comprised of only a few reading teachers at each school, with whom they work for consistent implementation of a core reading program, usually not beyond sixth grade.

The elementary literacy coach works on content reading strategies with a faculty of reading teachers with a much broader background knowledge of the five elements of reading. However, the secondary literacy coaches are working with a few reading teachers but with a majority of faculty who are teaching content reading strategies usually for comprehension, fluency, and vocabulary development.

Another difference between literacy coach experiences across grade levels is that elementary literacy coaches usually feel more welcome in the classroom from the beginning than their middle and high school counterparts. As a result, they can provide more classroom modeling sooner. In contrast, the middle and high school literacy coaches typically have to spend more time and work harder to gain this acceptance.

It is important to note that as struggling readers progress to higher grades, the achievement gap will widen. In other words, if a student is one grade level behind and has not been successfully remediated, that student may be more than one grade level behind at the end of the next year. As a result, the elementary literacy coach *must* have a strong background in early diagnosis and intervention strategies to immediately help these students. The secondary literacy coach must be well versed in intensive intervention and motivational strategies for struggling readers who may have fallen through the cracks. We believe that the basic function of the literacy coach is the same for all levels, but the background knowledge of the teachers varies, as do the developmental needs of the students. However similar the work, the amount of time spent in areas of coaching may differ.

WHAT IS LITERACY COACHING?

Literacy coaching is a service that enhances curriculum, instruction, assessment, professional development, resources, intervention, and community engagement to improve reading, writing, and content learning. Coaching may just be a short conversation sharing ideas with no formal follow up; or coaching may be much more complex and involve written plans, specific strategies, timelines, and so forth. Or, literacy coaching may be to outline a lesson infused with literacy strategies in a specific area such as comprehension. The literacy coach may aid with curriculum by helping teachers choose appropriate texts or lesson sequences. Offering a teacher tips and strategies for the delivery of a lesson, such as using graphic organizers to help the student link to prior knowledge, is an example of literacy coaching with an instructional focus.

The literacy coach may deliver whole or small group professional development to teach and model methods of differentiated instruction. An important part of the literacy coach's role is to offer up-to-date, research-based, professional development. The cornerstone of this is follow-up. Here is where we really see coaching at its finest. Just giving a *drive by* inservice will not help. The literacy coach is really coaching when following up with individual observations, modeling, conversations, feedback to the teacher, and so on. Coaching involves giving as much support as possible. We do not want the teacher to receive valuable information once, only to go back to the classroom and never try any of the new strategies. Furthermore, we want teachers to try the strategy, receive feedback from

Table 2.1   Literacy Coaching Service

Curriculum System Service Area	Example
Curriculum	Recommends enhancing reading of nonfiction text
Instruction	Recommends comprehension strategies, connecting to prior knowledge, KWL, etc.
Assessment	Assists with progress monitoring strategies, such as fluency probes
Professional Development	Offers mini-workshops during planning periods on differentiated instruction
Resources	Models fluency software, assists in selection of classroom libraries
Intervention	Assists the teacher for maximum time use and differentiated instruction
Parent/Community Engagement	Organizes and delivers parent/community literacy programs

KWL = know, want to know, learned.

an observation or conversation with the literacy coach, *and* work out the less successful areas and refine the technique.

In a good teacher-to-coach relationship, they both learn through the experience. Successful literacy coaches use what they have learned from other teachers' learning experiences to help more educators be successful. Constant support and monitoring is paramount to the coaching process. It is also important to remember that the successful coach must be flexible and able to recognize *coachable moments* in a variety of venues from the formal (workshops) to the informal (sidewalk chat).

SCENARIO: PROFESSIONAL DEVELOPMENT CLASSROOM RESULTS

Lake County, Florida, K–12 literacy coaches are an energetic professional learning community, but sometimes they are discouraged by the small gains made or grumblings from faculty members who are required to attend literacy professional development. Focusing on and sharing positive results like the one that follows keeps the momentum growing and should be placed in the literacy coach's professional portfolio. Recently, literacy coach Craig Cosden sent this e-mail:

> Dale,
>
> I just wanted to let you know that Mrs. Liverotti and I both tried your vocabulary activity in class this week; and we were thrilled

with the results. The students thoroughly enjoyed it. The raps and poems they (students) wrote surpassed my expectations. In my class I gave a pre- and posttest on the words used in the exercise; and saw a marked improvement in their scores. Thanks again for the great idea. It is refreshing to go to an inservice and come out with an activity that you can try right now with little effort, expense or materials which quickly reaps the benefits of learning. I really appreciate the positive energy you bring to EHS.

Kindest regards,

Amy

KNOWLEDGE, SKILLS, AND DISPOSITIONS

We have found that there are important threads of knowledge, skills, and dispositions for literacy coaching (see Table 2.2). The literacy coach must be, together with the school administrator, the literacy leader for the school. We strongly encourage the literacy coach to establish a literacy leadership team (LLT) for the school. We have found that this teacher leadership trait is the key to the literacy coach's success.

Literacy coaches must be well versed in the scientific research base of teaching reading and literacy infusion into content learning. The district and local administration must support the literacy coach's professional development to become this expert. The literacy coach's professional growth and relationship with administrators will be discussed in more detail later in this chapter, as well as in Chapters 5 and 9.

The last thread of knowledge, skills, and dispositions that effective literacy coaches possess is in working with adults through mentoring, small- and large-group professional development, and modeling literacy learning. Much like the coach of an athletic team, the literacy coach is the *go-to guy* to call the best strategy for a given situation.

Table 2.2 Knowledge, Skills, and Dispositions

Knowledge	Adult learning
	Literacy
	Assessment
Skills	Leadership
	Communication
Dispositions	Attitude of learning
	Collaboration

SCENARIO

A Literacy Coach Is Born

Several years ago, while teaching mathematics in a small Washington state school, Dale noticed that many students would do whatever they could to skip the word problems and not have to deal with them. They asked, "Just tell me, do I have to add, subtract, multiply, or divide these numbers?"

About halfway through the year, Dale welcomed two students from Vietnam into his class. Although they could not speak English, as he put the page numbers on the board and gave the assignment, they eagerly went to work with great accuracy. These Vietnamese students skipped the word problems just like their native born peers. It became painfully clear to Dale that the students' abilities to do mathematics were related to their reading ability.

Carol, an English teacher at the school, shared a planning period with Dale. Throughout the year, she gave Dale many tips to help the students comprehend the mathematics problems they were reading. As Dale began using the literacy strategies, not only did the Vietnamese students find mathematics success, but so did the other students! That year, the literacy coach was born for Dale.

Who Is Coached and How?

Determining who is coached and how is much like the scenario in *Good to Great* (Collins, 2001). The executives who ignited the transformations from good to great did not first figure out where to drive the bus and then get people to take it there. No, they first got the right people on the bus (and the wrong people off the bus) and figured out where to drive it. They said, in essence, "Look, I don't really know where we should take this bus. But I know this much: If we get the right people on the bus, the right people in the right seats, and the wrong people off the bus, then we'll figure out how to take it someplace great" (p. 41).

Who do you coach? Anyone willing to listen! We believe the *who* naturally divides itself into two groups. The first group is the across-all-content-areas group, which ranges from the elementary reading teacher to the high school English teacher, to the K–12 physical education teacher, to the advanced placement calculus teacher. The next group is those teaching K–12 intensive reading intervention students. This second group may include teachers of English as second language learners and teachers of special education students.

Why should you coach content area teachers? Think of it like teaching a schoolwide thematic unit in all content experiences. Imagine your school has a schoolwide thematic unit on westward expansion; and during mathematics instruction, the students compute the difference in distance traveled using a northern route and a southern route to the west. In language arts, they write a paragraph comparing and contrasting the challenges of taking a northern route as opposed to a southern route. During science instruction, different geological features are discussed, such as the differences in the mountain ranges that had to be crossed, weather patterns, and botanical differences. In social studies, the two different geographical cultures are topics each day. At the end of the unit, students have heard much about the two westward routes in a variety of ways, and the information is more likely to be retained in long-term memory.

The theory of all teachers using the same literacy strategies, just like all teachers working on a common thematic unit, works when implementing literacy strategies before, during, and after reading across the content areas. Teaching the students how to use literacy strategies before, during, and after reading in all content areas, day after day, helps embed them in their cognitive arsenals—ready to be called on when necessary. There is a cornerstone for raising student achievement in reading, writing, and content learning: embedding literacy strategies by consistently implementing nonnegotiable expectation of daily practice.

Yet, teachers may need additional literacy coaching to help the struggling readers in their classrooms, intensive reading intervention, or remedial reading classes. How do I design my classroom? Or, what does my class literacy time look like? These may be questions that the intensive reading or elementary teacher with below-grade-level readers needs answered. They benefit from the knowledge of literacy strategies but also need much more specific information about how best to develop phonics, phonemic awareness, vocabulary, fluency, and comprehension with struggling readers. Chapter 7 discusses specific support that the literacy coach may provide the intensive intervention teacher.

Again, the successful literacy coach develops a strong collaborative relationship with the intensive reading teacher and elementary teachers who have below-grade-level readers in their classes. Through this constant support, the literacy coach will observe strategies that work with particular struggling readers. This information can be shared with other teachers who have these students to help them understand what works for these particular readers. As a result, the teacher and students are strengthening their cognitive arsenal of literacy strategies for success.

We have learned from personal professional experience that the literacy coach cannot expect to reach everyone initially. Like all faculties and staff, some will be right on board and eager to have the literacy coach come into their classrooms and work with them. Some will have ideas and success stories that the literacy coach can use to help support other teachers. Others will allow the literacy coach to help them, but grudgingly. Finally, and sadly, some will not respond to the literacy coach at all. Our experience has shown that the literacy coach must concentrate on those who are eagerly willing at first. True, the literacy coach should offer coaching and professional development service to all faculty members but shouldn't worry about the resistant group. The successful literacy coach concentrates on the eager and willing and does not spend a lot of time trying to force the unwilling. As the culture of literacy grows in the school and the administrative leadership team provides literacy leadership, there will be many more supporters than resisters.

The coaching model combined with a fail-safe literacy process guarantees success. Once this achievement is evident, celebrate the successes and strive for more. Eventually the group in the middle will come around. Slowly, some of the most reluctant group will come around until you have the vast majority on your literacy team and working for the success of all students.

HOW ARE TEACHERS, STAFF, AND ADMINISTRATORS COACHED?

Next, the literacy coach should address how and when to coach as well as determine an appropriate service model. Many schools have either early student release days built into the school calendar or full days where professional development can take place. Other schools do not have either luxury and consider after school, before school, or even weekends. Schools have effectively delivered professional development in smaller groups during planning periods throughout the day. The successful literacy coach provides service in many different ways to reach each faculty member in the school. An overview of how coaching may be accomplished follows.

Large-Group Professional Development (Formal). In this case, the literacy coach is facilitating professional development to possibly the whole faculty. The coach may be doing the presentation alone or may have a consultant. In either case, the literacy coach is responsible for planning ahead and for planning follow-up over time.

Small-Group Professional Development (Formal). This professional development is similar to large group but takes place with much smaller groups, which may be teacher planning groups, grade levels, or departments.

Again, the literacy coach plans ahead for this presentation and will plan for follow-up activities. This model allows for much more feedback and interaction with the group, but the disadvantage is that the professional development must be repeated multiple times to reach the whole faculty.

Small-Group Professional Development (Informal). This is similar to the formal model, often happens spontaneously, and does not allow for planning time like the two formal models. In this case, a group of teachers may approach the coach with a question or concern. This is a coachable moment, and if possible the literacy coach responds on the spot. Sometimes informal small groups lead to more formal small-group presentations.

Modeling (Formal). In this case, the literacy coach either models literacy strategies or instruction in a professional development presentation or a teacher's classroom. Other teachers may also be included in watching the instruction. The follow-up would be for the coach to observe the teacher's implementation and offer suggestions and collaboration.

One-On-One (Informal or Formal). In the formal sense, one-on-one coaching involves a teacher wanting individual help or having individual concerns. For example, the science teacher may want to include more information on vocabulary development in the lessons. This can be informal when the teacher just stops in with a concern or question. The formal model involves working on a plan together until the teacher is comfortable and does not feel threatened. The coach may incorporate modeling or just give suggestions for the teacher to try. In either case, follow-up is important.

There are many other times when coachable moments will occur, and the successful literacy coach has the communication skills to take advantage of those opportunities. A discussion in the hallway or lounge indicating that a teacher may need help might lead to a simple one-on-one discussion and eventually more coaching. Students' academic performance may indicate a problem in a particular subject or grade level, which might lead to a coachable moment by having teachers get together to address the low scores.

Parents can and should also be included. Parents may be concerned with their children's progress and may come to the literacy coach for suggestions of things to do at home. The literacy coach may even go to the neighborhood or church and offer parent workshops. The important point here is that the successful literacy coach is always looking for the coachable moment, even creating opportunities, to reach the most people possible.

Remember, the literacy coach cannot force assistance on people. Work with those who express an interest first. When the others feel the sense of urgency and see the improvement in other classrooms, they will come around. If possible, design presentations that all faculty members will experience. Grumbling may be appear on the outside; but if they take back only one new idea and try it, you have been a success. Be patient, work hard with those who are receptive, and keep trying with those who are not. Literacy coaches are improving phonics, phonemic awareness, vocabulary, fluency, and comprehension of students, which will improve reading, writing, and content learning.

ROLES AND RESPONSIBILITIES

We rarely, if ever, have a literacy coach meeting without someone raising the concern about the massive scope of the job. "I am testing students all day and doing cafeteria duty, how can I truly be effective as a literacy coach?" We will address these specific concerns in more depth in Chapter 9 and offer a foundation here.

Before designing the roles and responsibilities of the literacy coach, it may be helpful to reflect on what others have identified as important. Recently, a list of literacy coach roles and responsibilities was created by an international group of 77 school and district administrators:

Smile and passion!

Availability

Flexibility

Research-based modeling, practices

The model for strategies for intervention

Responsible for professional development

Gradual release of responsibilities

Model for collaboration, making connections, climate builder

People skills

Credible—a part of what you present—experiences

Self-reflection

Assisting with data analysis

Answer the question, "Why?" (Taylor, 2004)

This list, created by a group of national and international practitioners, has clearly captured many of the expectations we mentioned.

While developing *Just Read, Lake!* (Taylor & Moxley, 2004), we convened groups of literacy coaches and administrators to develop the roles and responsibilities for the literacy coach. We felt that *Just Read, Lake!* would be unsuccessful if the literacy coach group created their own roles and responsibilities without working collaboratively with the administrators. This collaborative effort resulted in the following literacy coach roles and responsibilities:

a. Model the seven processes of literacy

b. Design and provide professional development

c. Lead the school literacy team

d. Work closely with administration and curriculum specialists

e. Maintain a professional library

f. Be willing and able to advise and assist teachers

g. Monitor progress

h. Promote the processes of literacy in the classrooms

i. Analyze student data

j. Stay abreast of current scientifically based reading research and best practices

k. Engage parents and the community in the literacy process

l. Promote reading motivation programs

m. Celebrate successes (p. 7)

We strongly believe that this process of collaboratively developing the roles and responsibilities with literacy coaches and administrators is an important ingredient for success. It is critical that both the coach and administrator understand the roles and responsibilities, and the best way to ensure that both groups have a mutual understanding of them is to create the expectations together. It is also wise to formally publish the literacy coach roles and responsibilities so they are readily available and visible. When implementing a literacy coach position, it is essential to be specific on the roles and responsibilities. This clarity provides direction for the coach, clarifies misconceptions, and provides a framework for monitoring and assessing the effectiveness of the position. The expectations, work, and assessment of the value of the literacy coach position at the school or district should be transparent.

REFLECTION

In our experience, literacy coaches who recognize and take advantage of coaching moments are successful and respected by the faculty, staff, and administration. Because literacy coaches are often not assigned students all day long, teachers may question their value; faculty may be resentful. The literacy coach who is not offended by such comments or queries and still makes every effort to smile and reach out to all faculty members will have a positive impact on student achievement. Together, even small steps in the right direction make a big difference in student achievement in a school or even in the district.

TERMS TO REMEMBER

Roles and responsibilities: Tasks for which the literacy coach is accountable.

Knowledge: What the literacy coach must know.

Skills: What the literacy coach must be able to do.

Dispositions: What attitudes the literacy coach communicates.

3 Preparing to Be a Literacy Coach

Surrender the me for the we.

(Jackson, p. 89)

Several years ago, Rose was responsible for developing literacy interventions for the lowest performing students in middle schools. It was difficult to find teachers who understood both reading and adolescents. It was even more difficult to find teachers who wanted to teach the lowest performing students. For three years, we evaluated the growth of students in these interventions to determine the most effective characteristics of the teachers and professional preparation. What we found may surprise you. The literacy intervention teachers with the greatest gains in student achievement had one thing in common: They were willing to attend all the professional development we provided, wanted to work with the neediest students, and agreed to faithfully implement the intervention as designed. Surprisingly, whether a teacher had a degree or background in reading had no correlation to improvement in student achievement!

How does this anecdote relate to preparation of literacy coaches? First, there is a shortage of literacy coaches! We regularly receive communications from colleagues asking if we know of any literacy coaches. In working with *Just Read, Lake!* and other district literacy initiatives, we found two necessary characteristics. First, the teacher must want to be a literacy coach to help teachers and students; second, the teacher must be willing to participate in the professional development provided (Taylor & Moxley, 2004). Few literacy coaches arrive at the position with knowledge, skills, and dispositions of collegial coaching, literacy, and leadership. In fact, in Sarasota County Public Schools, Florida, literacy coaches have been funded for all schools—elementary, middle, and high. To ensure that these literacy coaches are excellently prepared for their positions, the district has a weekly Friday session with all coaches to develop their knowledge of literacy, leadership, and coaching.

RECRUITING PROSPECTIVE LITERACY COACHES

Prospective literacy coach candidates with reading certification or reading endorsements are difficult to find. Often, the administrator must find someone willing to start in the literacy coach position and continue professional development toward a reading degree. The administrator must first determine that the prospective literacy coach is truly a *lifelong learner* with the desire to learn more about literacy and research-based practices for successful teaching.

The second major trait to look for is evidence that the prospective candidate can successfully work with others. The literacy coach must be able to work with new teachers and veterans alike.

How does the administrator go about finding these candidates? Attending recruiting or job fairs put on by local colleges is one possibility. Often, the well trained elementary teacher has a good background in literacy; and even though the administrator is at a secondary school, the elementary trained candidate may be a good fit. We also suggest looking within your own faculty for someone who has the respect of the other faculty and a love for literacy learning, a teacher-leader ready to take a new challenge.

DEVELOPING THE PROSPECTIVE LITERACY COACH

The prospective literacy coach's attitude must be, "Learn everything I can to be the best literacy coach possible for the faculty, staff, and administration." Some districts are offering systematic professional development on collegial coaching. Often, these professional development experiences are lead by the district literacy coach or another knowledgeable instructional leader. If you are in a small district, check with your regional service agency or state department of education for its scheduled professional development related to collegial coaching, instructional leadership, teacher leadership, and literacy. They may provide professional development for school-based and district-level literacy coaches. For example, Kentucky's state department of education provides literacy coach professional development for districts with Reading First grants for its primary grades. Recent useful publications are *How to Thrive as a Teacher Leader* (Gabriel, 2005) or the hallmark publication *Cognitive Coaching* (Costa & Garmston, 2002).

Most literacy coaches will be moving from a classroom teacher position and, unlike the principal, may not have a whole-school view. Even without schoolwide leadership experience, the literacy coach is selected because of the potential to lead. How can the literacy coach quickly get a whole-school perspective? Participation in whole-school decision-making and district committees related to literacy, student achievement, assessment, and finance will provide an important perspective and knowledge. Why finance? Literacy coaches will want to know all the avenues for seeking funds to provide support for literacy learning and how funding priorities are determined.

There are also excellent resources available online and in print from the International Reading Association, National Council of Teachers of English, Alliance for Excellent Education, Association for Supervision and Curriculum Development (ASCD), National Middle School Association, Phi Delta Kappa, and the principals' organizations. Potential literacy coaches should take time to collect resources, read, study, and think about their beliefs related to leading others and literacy learning. Publications that may help with this reflection include: *Leading With Character to Improve Student Achievement* (Williams & Taylor, 2003), *Literacy Leadership for Grades 5–12* (Taylor & Collins, 2003), and *The K–12 Literacy Leadership Fieldbook* (Taylor & Gunter, 2005). Rose is the coauthor of each of these resources, so they are consistent with the fail-safe literacy philosophy; each of these resources addresses literacy research and leadership.

Knowledge of scientific research-based literacy learning and the skill to model the research is essential. A good place to begin for elementary coaches is the *Report of the National Reading Panel: Teaching Children to Read* (National Institute of Child Health and Human Development, 2000) and *Preventing Reading Difficulties in Young Children* (Snow, Burns, & Griffin, 1998). Middle and high school coaches should consider *Reading Next: A Vision for Action and Research in Middle and High School Literacy* (Biancarosa & Snow, 2004). Without internalized knowledge and skill of literacy learning, literacy coaches cannot effectively teach, model, and practice to lead teachers. In Chapter 4, professional books for the literacy coach's library are identified. These texts should be read by the literacy coach first, and shared with others. Like students, teachers should become experts in content before helping students acquire competence in content knowledge.

Obviously, the content knowledge of the literacy coach is reading, writing, and literacy learning along with literacy assessment and use of assessment data to improve achievement. Additionally, essential content knowledge includes effective classroom practice and homework. Many common practices in school have little gain; giving homework as an introduction to content and concepts is not as effective as assigning homework for independent practice after introduction and guided practice in class. For more on this research, *What Works in Schools* (Marzano, 2003) and *Classroom Instruction That Works* (Marzano, Pickering, & Pollock, 2001) provide a quick research-based background on instruction that yields more gain than other instruction. Assessment will be discussed in depth in Chapter 6.

For expertise in reading, a recent graduate degree in reading may help if it was a high quality experience and aligned with the most current research on literacy learning and student achievement. Some states provide online professional development in reading free of charge. Large districts usually provide reading modules or reading and writing professional development that is free to teachers and literacy coaches.

If these free sources are unavailable, nonprofit organizations like International Reading Association (IRA) and ASCD offer professional development related to literacy and literacy leadership, which may be online or at preconference institutes, conferences, or stand-alone institutes. Remember, becoming familiar with the organizations' Web sites and services will support the literacy coaches in their own professional development. We encourage coaches to attend the local, regional, state, and national conferences; and on returning to the district and school, we urge them to share what they learned.

Besides public education and nonprofit professional development, most literacy-related publishers offer professional development, many of which are online. Look for resources with strands for teachers, literacy coaches, and administrators. Potential coaches are encouraged to investigate possibilities for themselves, as well as for fellow teachers, for participation in these kinds of literacy learning opportunities.

Boost confidence by taking advantage of available resources to confirm what the literacy coach knows, and remind the coach of the current research base on literacy learning. There will be difficult days and naysayers, so literacy coaches must have confidence in their knowledge and skills. The term *fail-safe literacy* connotes success. It is an approach of the knowledgeable, skillful professional with the disposition to be effective.

OBTAINING CERTIFICATION OR ENDORSEMENT AS A LITERACY COACH

Potential literacy coaches will want to consult with their district personnel department or state department of education about any coursework offered or required to be a literacy coach. Florida requires that literacy coaches complete a sequence of courses that results in a reading endorsement for their teaching certificate beginning in July 2006. This could determine whether or not a potential literacy coach pursues the position.

Chapter 2 identified dispositions literacy coaches should have, including positive relationships with faculty and the ability to listen and coach them.

No matter how great the knowledge and skill of an educator, without mutually respectful relationships with the faculty, staff, and administration the literacy coach will be ineffective.

Furthermore, the literacy coach should have the disposition for collaboration. Collaborating within the school as well as with other literacy coaches enhances success. The coach who wants to tell, rather than listen and problem solve, will not have long-term success either within a school or within a district. A helpful resource for reflecting on collaboration and literacy learning is *Systems for Change in Literacy Education* by Lyons and Pinnell (2001).

Our experience with the literacy coaches in Lake County and other districts confirms that they add value to each other through their willingness to collaborate and support one another. Through this collaborative experience, their knowledge and skills continually develop to produce outstanding respected experts. Feedback from literacy coaches indicates this is important. At each collaborative session, Dale allowed time for coaches to work in neighborhood school feeder patterns or job-alike groups. In school feeder patterns, an elementary school sends students to a specific middle school that sends students to a particular high school, and those educators meet together. In job-alike groups, elementary literacy coaches meet together, as do middle school coaches and high school coaches. Job-alike groups may also be for those working on a particular professional development module or assessment. Literacy coaches are one another's best resources since they understand the families and the school context.

DEVELOPING CREDIBILITY AND CONFIDENCE

Think about the go-to person for any concern you have. How do you select that individual? Most likely, you go to the most credible person and the person in whom you have confidence; the effective literacy coach will be both.

As discussed in Chapter 2, credibility with the faculty, staff, and administration is a prerequisite for the position. However, there are many literacy coaches who are new to a school or who were elementary teachers and now find themselves in the challenging position of high school literacy coach. Either way, the first step is to establish credibility with those who are served. Credibility is developed more by actions than words, so the wise literacy coach will leave the résumé in the drawer.

Words to the shrewd literacy coach: listen, listen, listen. It highlights, "I respect you and want to know who you are and how I can assist you." During the listening sessions, needs or questions will always arise. Credibility will develop with swift, respectful responses. In other words, immediately develop a mutually respectful relationship, provide service, and follow through—no matter what else comes up. The literacy coach who develops a reputation for being in the office, working on the computer, or being away from the school campus will probably find the position quickly eliminated. Walk the walk.

Credibility develops as the literacy coach provides mini-workshops, resources, and coaching tips. As the literacy coach models before, during, and after reading strategies for a teacher *and the strategies work,* the word will spread: The coach is a great resource! Likewise, as the literacy coach works closely with the reading intervention teacher and the lowest 25% of the students show improved reading, credibility with the teacher and administration will be enhanced. Credibility cements the value of the position and helps eliminate negative attributions. The literacy coach is a service provider, and the more service provided *with results,* the greater the credibility.

SCENARIO

Role Model District Literacy Coach

In Logan County, Kentucky, there is a district role model literacy coach, Elisa Beth Brown. As a district literacy coach, her first priority is working with Reading First elementary schools, then other elementary schools, and then remaining middle grades and the high schools. Although each elementary school has resource specialists, such as Title I specialists, they still call on this new literacy coach for support.

One of the Title I elementary schools invited Elisa Beth to provide service. After several visits, the teachers began to implement her suggestions. In January of that school year, Rose visited this elementary school and conducted literacy walkthroughs in each of the K–8 classrooms. Using a Classroom Guide for Literacy (Form 3.1), some observations generated recommendations; but there were also positive observations, including reader's theater, word walls with content focus, smooth transitions, and effective use of centers.

In the debrief with the faculty and administration, Rose shared the positive observations as well as some ideas to consider. Without provocation, the teachers made it clear that Elisa Beth was exceptional and everything that she had suggested, including reader's theater, was working well. These teachers gave Elisa Beth great accolades for her positive respectful approach, relationship with the teachers, and credibility. Unaware that Rose knew and was working with the Elisa Beth, the teachers' comments were genuine and gracious; they were clearly desirous of more literacy coaching.

Form 3.1 Classroom Guide for Literacy PreK–12

You may use this form for self-monitoring, identifying areas for growth, and making your professional development plan. Also, ask for input from a colleague or the literacy coach. Check the box for each line that best represents your classroom.

The classroom has . . .	N	P	RM	Action Plan
Literacy rich and print rich environment				
Differentiated instruction and stations				
Attractive, risk-free environment				
Smooth schedule, groups, transitions				
Student-known routines, resources				
Maximized time for literacy learning				
Integration of literacy content with curriculum standards				
Celebration of learning				
The teacher . . .	**N**	**P**	**RM**	**Action Plan**
Incorporates the seven processes of literacy				
Incorporates critical thinking strategies				
Models joy of reading to and with students daily				
Provides daily accountable independent reading K-12				
Assists students in selecting reading materials				
Promotes reading of nonfiction				
Monitors reading improvement with student data				
Teaches, models, and practices before, during, and after literacy strategies				

N = novice; P = proficient. RM = role model.

SOURCE: Taylor, R. T., & Gunter, G. A., p. 115. Used with permission.

PROMOTING LITERACY LEARNING, NOT YOURSELF

Readers may be wondering why this section exists. Let us share a scenario from a literacy coach meeting.

SCENARIO

Self-Promotion

Literacy coaches from elementary, middle, and high schools are present for their monthly meeting and collaboration. They have worked and grown together for more than two years and consider themselves a learning community. Whenever one of them creates a new mini-workshop or discovers a research-based resource, it is shared with all the rest. One person's success is everyone's success.

During this particular monthly session, there is a relatively new literacy coach sitting in the front row who appears to be taking notes on her laptop. She is busy and periodically makes a comment or poses a question to the speaker. The speaker wonders what she is saying that could possibly generate that many notes but continues on with the day's agenda.

At the lunch break, a veteran literacy coach is fuming! She shares that the newer literacy coach sitting in the front row is working on her graduate class assignments. Unfortunately, the graduate work is toward gaining school administration certification. To the veteran literacy coach, the newcomer is a traitor using the literacy coach position to impress the principal, accentuate her value, and be appointed as an assistant principal. The veteran literacy coach is proud of what the literacy coaches had accomplished and their collectively positive credibility related to improving reading, writing, and content learning.

We are both former principals and district administrators and supportive of novice administrators and those who wish to become administrators. Still, potential literacy coaches should heed this scenario. The relationships within and outside of the school are critical to the literacy coach position and impact on student achievement. Perception of using the literacy coach position for personal gain—rather than for gain in reading, writing, and content learning—will undermine relationships and credibility with faculty, staff, and administration.

In *Sacred Hoops,* Jackson (1995) discussed how coaching a high performing team with the likes of Michael Jordan is a tremendous challenge. This same kind of challenge exists in schools: Many teachers are superstars and so is the literacy coach. Assisting these superstars to embrace the belief that through collaboration the students achieve more as do all the faculty, staff, and administration will assist in creating a school culture of literacy. The successful literacy coach surrenders the me for the we!

REFLECTION

We have observed literacy coaches in a variety of settings—rural, urban, suburban. All effective literacy coaches have positive relationships with the faculty, staff, and administration. Credibility with knowledge and skills develops along with and after the relationship is established. Literacy coaching is a service; it is about we, not me.

TERMS TO REMEMBER

Walkthrough: A literacy coach, administrator, or other valued colleague may walk through classrooms and remain five to ten minutes. During these literacy focused walkthroughs, the coach will note specific positive literacy behaviors and things on which to coach the teacher.

Personal gain: This motivation is perceived as for personal recognition or promotion, rather than for the good of the students, teachers, or school.

Knowledge: What we cognitively own is knowledge.

Skills: This refers to what we do.

Dispositions: Attitude, behavioral style, leadership style combine to form our dispositions.

4 Getting Ready to Provide Literacy Coaching Service

Literacy Coach . . . serves as a resource in the areas of reading and writing instruction, assessment in cooperation with other professionals, and diagnosis of students at one or more of the following levels: early childhood, elementary, middle, secondary, or adult.

(International Reading Association, 2004a, p. 7)

We have discussed who literacy coaches are (the teacher-leader responsible for promoting and enhancing literacy instruction with the ultimate goal of improving student achievement as measured by reading, writing, and content learning) and the expectations that districts and schools have for them. As the International Reading Association (IRA) quote from *Standards for Reading Professionals* suggests, literacy coaches are service providers. Now it is time to prepare for effective delivery, which includes appropriate work space, resources, personal preparation, and planning.

After the appointment to the position, the hard work begins: preparing to provide literacy coaching services to faculty, staff, students, parents, and the administration. As we worked with new literacy coaches over the last several years, a roadmap helped accelerate service related to improving literacy and content learning. These literacy coaches spent much of their first year following our recommendations. This chapter is intended to provide practical guidance for the literacy coach preparing to provide service and to get started quickly.

WORK SPACE

Those in leadership know that how physical space is allocated and used in a school is in direct proportion to the perceived value of the service. The literacy coach and principal should discuss the need for both office and professional development space. These can be two different spaces or a shared space. Either way, the message of the space allocation should be clear: Literacy and content learning are priorities in the school.

Often, the literacy coach space is next to the media center or in a professional development center near the school's administrative offices. Keep in mind that the space is a resource area, not a destination. These are purposeful locations that work well to provide literacy service to teachers and communicate effectively with the administration. Media centers are positive locations because of the availability of both print and nonprint resources. The media specialist is critical to the improvement of literacy achievement; literacy coach space nearby encourages both formal and informal interaction between the two positions, as well as mutual support.

A nonexample of a literacy coach space would be converted custodial closet (which we have seen) or a space inconvenient for teacher and administrator access, perhaps at the back of the school. When this takes place, literacy coaches typically do not have adequate workspace or, in particular, professional development and coaching space.

Excellent classroom teachers are strategic about their use of classroom space. The same goes for the excellent literacy coach. Space is purposefully and deliberately arranged and used. There are many ways that effective literacy coaches can organize their resources.

Think about the items that follow. What purpose does each serve? How does each relate to the roles and responsibilities discussed in Chapter 2? Keep in mind that structure supports goal attainment. The goal is improved student achievement through literacy learning. Everything within the space should speak to the purposeful and deliberate work to achieve the school's goal.

- Office and technology workstation
- Bookcases for professional books
- Bookcases for student resources
  - Read alouds, picture books, poetry, fiction, nonfiction
  - Examination texts
- Publisher catalogs of appropriate resources
- Small-group area for mini-workshops or study groups
- Technology for professional development
  - Laptop
  - Liquid crystal display (LCD) projector

- o Overhead projector
- o Laser pointer
- o Desktop computer
- o Printer, scanner, fax
- o Digital camera
- o Projector for opaque objects
- Supply cabinet
  - o Markers
  - o Transparencies
  - o Transparency pens
  - o Chart paper
  - o Note cards
  - o Note pads
  - o Pens
  - o Pencils
- Evidence of student work with rubrics
- Photos of teachers engaged in literacy learning
- Photos of students engaged in literacy learning
- Assessment materials
- Data charts of student achievement
- Refreshment area

TECHNOLOGY

Appropriate technology is essential for the effective literacy coach. When invited into a school to support literacy learning, we are surprised when locating a workable overhead projector is a challenge, or it is a major ordeal for a power point presentation to be shared. The conclusion is that if the invited guest does not have access to appropriate technology, then the literacy coach does not have it on a day-to-day basis. This lack of appropriate technology sends the wrong message to the faculty and staff regarding the importance of literacy learning and professional development.

Basic technology for a professional development provider, a literacy coach, has to be up-to-date and accessible within the workspace. At least have an office computer that scans and faxes and a printer. When we are in a school, a teacher or literacy coach frequently has questions about resources needed for a specific group of students. A quick search of the Internet reveals the publisher's or organization's Web sites, and potential resources and solutions become a reality.

For workshops and modeling literacy learning, a laptop computer, projector, and laser pointer are necessities. A poor quality projector is useless and frustrating for the presenter as well as the participants. Overhead projectors are a good standby and effective as long as the focus is sharp. A good backup plan for presentations is to have a set of transparencies in case the computer projector does not work. Recently, a literacy session of extremely high importance took place with highly placed decision makers. After fumbling with technology that did not work and frustrating the decision makers, the presenter tried to recover. Unfortunately, the impact was lost and the presenter had no backup plan.

You may be wondering why the technology list contains a scanner, projector for opaque objects (such as an Elmo), and digital camera. The scanner is invaluable for showing examples of both student and teacher work as well as literacy resources. A projector for sharing books, student work, and teacher work can be equally valuable to project pages from a text; it will share concrete as well as transparent images. Digital cameras of high enough quality to take photos of classrooms, teachers, and students for incorporation into presentations can make the literacy learning applicable in the context of the school's specific environment. These resources help the literacy coach model and create mental models of excellent literacy learning.

The literacy coach needs workspace and the technology to model excellence in literacy learning for the faculty, staff, and administration. Literacy coaches should not have to borrow or search for necessary equipment. Keep in mind that the allocation of personnel for literacy coaching should be supported with the resources, technology, and budget to provide literacy coaching service.

PROFESSIONAL RESOURCES

As a resource provider, it is essential that the literacy coach have contemporary, relevant texts for teacher reading, literacy coach reading, and references to support research-based literacy practice. Review the reference list and other resources of this text for ideas for building your professional resource library. Subscribing to professional journals like *The Reading Teacher, Reading Research Quarterly,* and *Journal of Adolescent and Adult Literacy* will serve the literacy coach well. Other subscriptions that we recommend are for *Phi Delta Kappan* and *Educational Leadership.*

Studying the Web sites of publishers such as Corwin Press will alert the literacy coach to new publications. They have wonderful professional resources to support the work of the literacy coach. *Why Kids Can't Read: What Teachers Can Do* by Kylene Beers (2003) and *I Read It, But I Don't Get It* by Cris Tovani (2000) are favorites for teacher study groups. *Subjects Matter* by Harvey Daniels and Steven Zemelman (2004) and *Strategies That Work* by Stephanie Harvey and Anne Goudvis (2000) continue to be excellent research-based teacher and literacy coach resources. Their work is consistent with fail-safe literacy.

Keep in mind that every resource should be research based. So, the literacy coach should consider publications from the Educational Research Service like *Effective Early Reading Instruction* (Wilson & Protheroe, 2002), *What We Know About: Helping Struggling Learners in the Elementary and Middle Grades* (Protheroe, Shellard, & Turner, 2004), and *Reading at the Middle and High School Levels: Building Active Readers Across the Curriculum* (Wilson, 2004). Each is short, to the point, and easy to understand. These resources are inexpensive, less than $20 each, because they are published by a nonprofit organization. Literacy coaches should have research to support the use of the aforementioned texts, which are more teacher friendly with scenarios in classrooms.

All resource texts should be ordered in at least sets of two—one for the literacy coach and one for faculty, staff, and administration to check out. For those that will be the focus for teacher study groups, order 10, and allow the teachers to keep the text at the end of the study for personal reference.

STUDENT TEXTS

Think about the purpose of having student texts in the literacy coach space. What are some possible reasons? These are the basic reasons for having respectful student texts on the bookshelves and attractively displayed:

- Texts can be used as resources for modeling literacy strategies.
- Texts provide opportunities to examine new or supplementary texts.

The literacy coach will also want to have the content-area textbooks used by teachers to model research-based strategies before, during, and after reading with teachers.

Part of the literacy coach's role is to market or introduce appropriate supplemental texts to teachers that support both literacy and content learning. *Scope Magazine* (middle school), *Time for Kids* (elementary), and *Upfront* (Nebhum, Ed.) (high school) are supplemental texts that address literacy and content learning in a respectful context. Beyond magazines, there are excellent resources for the struggling reader, such as *Sourcebook* (Pavlik & Ramsey, 2000) or *Reader's Handbook* (Robb, 2002). On occasions, we have found these resources in schools unused until they were modeled by the literacy coach for faculty. On returning to the school a few weeks later, the teachers expressed how well the resources were working with their students and how the students enjoyed them.

Additionally, the literacy coach should have a model classroom library of student texts that covers reading ranges, genres, interests, and developmental stages. This model is a resource for workshops and modeling use of fiction and nonfiction to engage students, teach vocabulary and fluency, model strategies, and develop comprehension. *Because of Winn Dixie* (DiCamillo, 2000), *Holes* (Sachar, 1998), and the *Bluford Series* (2004) are contemporary texts that engage teacher and students alike. Besides prose, do not forget poetry, like a *Joyful Noise*, a book of science poetry for two voices by Paul Fleischman (1988). Displaying texts by one author, like Patricia Polacco, is also an effective way to model for teachers.

SCENARIO

Classroom Author Display

As I entered the second grade classroom, the students were engaged in reader's theater. The teacher learned about reader's theater from the district literacy coach as a way to motivate reading, enhance comprehension, and build fluency. One of the print rich characteristics of this classroom was a large display of books by Patricia Polacco. This engaging display included *Pink and Say* (1994), *The Keeping Quilt* (1998), *Thunder Cake* (1990), and *Butterfly* (2000). This historical fiction was visually supported in the classroom. Although the print rich display was beautiful and added visual interest, it also motivated students to engage with and learn about the history strand in the texts.

Does the model classroom library make a difference? Do literacy coaches influence which student texts are used by faculty? Read the two e-mails that were sent to Dale from literacy coaches and draw your own conclusion.

From Nancy Schiavone, teacher at Eustis High School:

Mr. E, the reading coach, thought you might be interested in knowing this. I have a class of ESE (special education) Life Management students who are very difficult. They hate everything. I told them a couple of days ago we would start "silent reading" for 15 minutes each day. I showed them the *Bluford* books I have in the room. The result was: they wouldn't stop reading! I told them we would extend the time a little. Finally, they said they would like to get the regular work over with today and went on to the lesson. Now they come in every day, pick up their books and READ. The *Bluford* books changed the whole class.

From Pat Fisher, Literacy Coach Umatilla High School:

I am so excited. I ordered 100 *Bluford* books for Tammie Henry, one of our reading intervention teachers. She was going to read them with her students as a class. Well, when they came in, the kids, jaded juniors and senior students, went crazy for them. One student said, "I know you love us Mrs. Henry because you got us books with black people in them." How powerful. They have checked these books out to read over the holidays. We are making a difference.

As the literacy coach develops the model classroom library, the coach will be sure to incorporate a listening center and audiobooks. Audiobooks can be on tape or compact disks and can be purchased or recorded by fluent volunteers. Either way, they are excellent resources for providing a fluent model for below-grade-level readers and for providing access to on-grade-level texts for those students who do not read on grade level. Keep in mind that these student texts are instructive, because students can access content about two years above their independent reading level with fluent reading support. Our point of view is that unabridged texts are the best as they model well-formed sentences and beautiful language and are not demeaned in any way. An excellent resource for the literacy coach is Recorded Books, which can be found at www.recordedbooks.com. Audiobooks and books on compact disks are consistent with the nonnegotiable expectation of daily practices, providing modeling for all grade levels. Modeling is recommended for developing fluency, joy of reading, and motivating reading (Wilson & Protheroe, 2002; Biancarosa & Snow, 2004).

Since reading achievement is measured in both fiction and nonfiction, be sure to include high quality nonfiction related to the content curriculum. This inclusion will encourage the content teachers to incorporate literacy learning into their daily instruction and not see it as the language arts teacher's responsibility. Do not assume that teachers know how to joyfully engage students either with their content textbook or with other texts to improve reading, writing, and content learning.

BUDGET

As you can see from the previous sections, the literacy coach needs a budget. Create a matrix of the kinds of resources needed for the work and professional development. List each item, its use, and its estimated expense. Provide this matrix along with rationale (such as we have provided) to your principal for approval and inclusion in the school's budget. Besides the resources included in the chapter, literacy coaches will want an account for supporting teachers with purchases as the need arises.

SCENARIO

Resource Coaching

Rose was talking with a teacher who works with high school at-risk students who read below grade level. The teacher was struggling with motivating students to read and with the resources available to her. Rose introduced her to the *Bluford Series*, adolescent literature whose main characters are African American. The teacher thought the series sounded perfect for her students, but did not know how to acquire them. The assistant principal immediately confirmed the purchase when it was requested. Within minutes, the commitment was made to purchase the *Bluford Series*, and the teacher was excited to be receiving resources respectful of her students.

Besides the *Bluford Series* for accountable independent reading, Rose pointed out that the *Sourcebook* (Pavlik & Ramsey, 2000) was available on the literacy coach's bookshelf and was designed for below-grade-level readers. The *Sourcebook* is organized with before, during, and after reading strategies; focuses on nonfiction; and is consumable.

Furthermore, the teacher had plans to teach *Romeo and Juliet* later in the spring—knowing that it was part of the district curriculum. Students enjoy the themes (drugs, sex, love, violence, gangs) but cannot read Shakespeare. During the conversation, Rose reached over to the shelf where copies of the *Reader's Handbook* (Robb, 2002) were stored and turned to the drama section. The section on drama specifically discussed introducing Shakespeare's *Romeo and Juliet*. There were more resources in the teacher's guide to the *Reader's Handbook*. Armed with appropriate adolescent resources and professional resources to accomplish what she wanted to do, the teacher left encouraged that she would assist the students in remaining in school, *and* they would joyfully be engaged in the second semester work.

This is an example of how the literacy coach can assist teachers—the moment of need should not pass without action being taken. Literacy coaches must have the knowledge, skills, dispositions, and resources to offer support for specific needs. Rose has found that if the literacy coach does not act immediately or claims a lack of resources, the teachers become demotivated and do not move forward with acquisition and improved literacy learning.

CALENDAR

Any professional without a class schedule with assigned students throughout the day is going to be scrutinized by the remainder of the faculty. This includes the literacy coach. We recommend that literacy coaches make a monthly calendar, post it on the work space door, and e-mail it to the faculty, staff, and administration. Let everyone know what days you are doing workshops and classroom visits, modeling literacy learning, having study groups, attending district meetings, or are available for coaching on planning periods.

A systematic calendar will probably work best. As an example, on Mondays and Fridays, the literacy coach may be in the office available for individual or team coaching. On Wednesdays, perhaps mini-workshops are offered on planning periods. On Tuesdays, the literacy coach is modeling in classrooms, and on Thursdays coaching teachers in classrooms. Regular meetings with the principal and administrative team, grade-level groups, and departments should also be on the calendar.

Assessment of students and data study will be part of the literacy coach role. Be sure to include assessment and data study on the calendar. Further detail on data study is provided in Chapter 6. The entire faculty will be amazed at how much time assessment and data study take. In Lake County, Florida, the literacy coaches serving teachers in elementary, middle, and high schools spent an average of 30% of their time with assessment and data use (Taylor & Moxley, 2004). Teachers will be pleased to have assistance with understanding student achievement data and using it to make instructional decisions.

The literacy coach will find that the calendar is full. By creating and communicating a calendar, the literacy coach's visibility and literacy focus will be reinforced. Regular communication with the calendar to the administration and faculty will help them fully understand the literacy coach's role and how the service is provided.

ESSENTIAL CORE PROFESSIONAL DEVELOPMENT

Before the school year begins and after studying student and teacher literacy achievement data, the literacy coach should think about the professional development most needed by the faculty, staff, and administration. A strategy that works well in Lake County Schools, Florida, is for the literacy coaches to work together to develop Essential Core Professional Development Modules. These modules are shared with faculty, staff, and administration each month on planning periods, before school, after school, and on Wednesdays, when students have a shortened school day. By providing the Essential Core Professional Development modules, a base of essential literacy learning knowledge is gained by teachers and administrators. Providing workshops represents about 13% of literacy coaches' time K–12 (Taylor & Moxley, 2004).

In Seminole County Schools, Florida, high school literacy coaches are using a different model for essential professional development. They have identified key professional development topics. All high school literacy coaches attend professional development on these key topics, then pairs of coaches volunteer to transfer the learning into a module to deliver to specific content teachers from all six high schools at the same time. This means that all literacy coaches have background knowledge and support the essential literacy infusion with teachers in their schools. However, each pair further develops at least six professional development modules and delivers them on given days in one location, perhaps to all ninth-grade science teachers in the district. This way, the delivery is content specific.

With both examples, the results in teacher change and student achievement have been positive. Therefore, we encourage literacy coaches to plan and calendarize those essential core professional development modules, mini-workshops, or days that are appropriate for the faculty, staff, and administration based on data-driven needs. More details about delivering meaningful professional development will be shared in Chapter 8.

SCENARIO

Providing Resources With Technology

At a large, diverse high school, Lyman High School, the literacy coach is a new position. Teachers are concerned about their class sizes and wonder if the position is really necessary. Fortunately, the literacy coach is a former reading intervention teacher in this same school. Tillie Steele was invited to become the literacy coach because of the gains her students made in reading and her positive relationship with the faculty.

Getting ready for the first year as literacy coach, she was given a large room next to the media center. Tillie has designed her space with her work in mind: bookshelves of professional and student texts, presentation and coaching area in the center, and her office workspace at the end of the room. A refreshment area is also in the room with a coffee pot and small refrigerator. Tillie knows that when she has mini-workshops or coaching, offering a little refreshment encourages participation and assists with the relationship building.

Although this new literacy coach is just getting started, Tillie committed to using technology to reach the large faculty. E-mail is a regular mode of communication, but she also set up a folder on the school's server for literacy resources. In the folder, Tillie places graphic organizers, notes from meetings, links to important Web sites, and other literacy resources. This innovative approach has hooked many of the faculty who go to the folder when planning their instruction to enhance the literacy and content learning.

As a first year literacy coach, Tillie is a successful, credible resource to the faculty, staff, and administration. They seek her out for personal literacy coaching, resources, and support with data-driven decision making. Her quick start as a successful literacy coach is because of her purposeful and deliberate actions to prepare to provide literacy coaching service.

REFLECTION

During the last several years, we have supported the implementation of literacy coach positions, their preparation, and success. We have also monitored their work and related their actions to positive changes in student achievement. Those literacy coaches who get ready to provide literacy coaching service lose no time in serving teachers, rapidly gain teacher trust, and have a measurable difference in student achievement in reading, writing, and content learning.

TERMS TO REMEMBER

Adolescent literature: This literature relates to the themes adolescents enjoy with adolescents as main characters.

Essential core professional development: This professional development is designed to provide a base of literacy knowledge for faculty, staff, and administration.

Literacy coaching service: Literacy coaches are service providers. Literacy coaches should prepare themselves to provide purposeful and deliberate service to improve student achievement.

Modules: Modules are professional development units.

Mini-workshops: These workshops can last anywhere from 45 minutes to 1 hour.

Read alouds: Texts for a teacher to read aloud to students while they listen.

Supplemental texts: These texts support literacy development and content learning in addition to the core text.

5 Building the Literacy Team

Teachers should assume leadership roles and spearhead curricular improvements.

(Biancarosa & Snow, 2004, p. 21)

Although the literacy coach can be an essential part of improving student achievement, one person cannot make the gains alone. There have always been exemplary teachers who consistently implemented research-based instructional practice. Rather than a few teachers being exemplary, the purposefully and deliberately created schoolwide literacy team infuses consistent, research-based practice throughout the school. The schoolwide student achievement growth only takes place with consistent, research-based instruction and monitored instruction with data study (Chapter 6) to further inform instructional decisions. Since the literacy coach is not directly teaching the students, the only way to make significant impact on student achievement is by collaboratively working with and through others. In this chapter, we discuss the Literacy Leadership Team (LLT), as well as the schoolwide literacy team of the entire faculty, and the vital team players beyond the school. Benefits of extending the reach of the literacy coach beyond the school and district also are addressed.

LITERACY LEADERSHIP TEAM

We encourage each district and school to develop its own LLT. The school LLT should be lead by the principal and the literacy coach. The LLT should have representatives for every grade level and content area. At a minimum, representatives from the administration, core reading, reading intervention, language arts or English, science, social studies, mathematics, library media center, and electives should be included. Since reading comprehension standardized assessments have items from science and social studies, these content teachers should be included. Mathematics teachers should be included because the most difficult area on mathematics assessments for students typically is the reading portions, word problems, or extended responses. Parents, students, district administrators, university partners, or business partners may also help (Taylor & Gunter, 2005).

Who in the school has influence over books purchased? Who uses them? The librarian media specialist—perhaps the most critical partner for the literacy coach and participant on the LLT. Helping these professionals understand their work's value, their influence on student reading, and their influence on teacher use of resources should be addressed directly by the literacy coach and LLT. Research by Baumbach (2004) supports the positive influence of the librarian media specialist on student reading, particularly the influence on the growth in reading achievement in elementary, middle, and high schools. According to Baumbach, influence on student achievement has been documented to be as much as 6% in high schools, depending on the work of the librarian media specialist. More information on the impact on student achievement through the librarian media specialists' work can be found at www.sunlink.ucf.edu/makingthegrade.

Some of the most important members of the LLT represent the arts and athletic endeavors. Why do we encourage participation by these teachers rather than just core reading teachers or reading intervention teachers? The answer lies in the relationship that elective, exploratory, and cocurricular teachers have with students. These professionals often have the biggest influence on the students who struggle the most. Having such professionals on the LLT gives all teachers and students a voice and makes everyone know that they have a substantial role to play in improving reading, writing, and content learning in the school.

The literacy coach has an important role in assisting with LLT development. After the team has been developed with volunteers and others invited, the purpose and work should be set forth by the principal and literacy coach. We recommend studying research on literacy learning that is developmentally appropriate for the students in the school, studying data (Chapter 6), and developing a school or district fail-safe literacy system. The literacy system should address curriculum, instruction, assessment, professional development, resources, intensive reading intervention, and parent and community engagement. (For assistance with developing a fail-safe literacy system, consider *The K–12 Literacy Leadership Fieldbook* [Taylor & Gunter, 2005]). Literacy coaches should define a

SCENARIO

Engaging Those Who Influence Students

When visiting an excellent school that recently set literacy learning as a priority, I noticed a huge banner hanging in the back of the school cafeteria that read, "Courtyard Café." When I asked about the Courtyard Café, I learned that the art teacher supports literacy learning with art students researching contemporary diverse authors and their works. As they learn about these authors and their works, they develop beautiful literacy-related murals on the courtyard walls. This area is now a literacy courtyard, created by the art teacher and art students, where students go to read at lunchtime.

literacy system and its key parts to ensure that every student and teacher is touched.

Once the LLT is organized and has its purpose set forth, making a calendar to support the work is essential. Many LLTs retreat for several days in the summer (with pay) to write or update the annual literacy system and implementation plan. During the retreat, they plan the opening professional development for the faculty, staff, and administration and make a calendar of professional development options for the school year. With the LLT collaborating on the calendar and offerings, participation will increase because of the increased schoolwide advocacy.

Following the summer retreat, regularly scheduled update sessions are vital for the LLT to keep literacy learning in the forefront of everyone's agenda. When the literacy coach, principal, and LLT carefully plan systematic leadership, schoolwide literacy infusion and support will flourish for literacy coaching service delivery.

The literacy coach must play a major role in building the LLT. Administrators are called out for meetings and other emergencies preventing them from attending every LLT meeting. The literacy coach must ensure that meetings are regularly scheduled and take place. The literacy coach should actively recruit members for the team who can make an impact, such as the media specialist. Providing refreshments can help the LLT look forward to and possibly inspire others to attend the meetings. The literacy coach should strive to create a working and influential team. Whenever something concerning literacy is on the agenda with a decision that will directly involve the literacy process, the literacy coach should encourage the administrator to have the LLT address the problem.

BEYOND THE LITERACY LEADERSHIP TEAM

As we have recommended, the LLT is a starting point for collaborative development, implementation, and monitoring of the school or district's fail-safe literacy system. These participants have spheres of influence beyond the LLT in departments, grade levels, and on other committees where literacy infusion can advance within the school and district. As more professionals use the same language and advocate the same professional practice, the school or district culture becomes one of cohesive literacy learning (rather than disparate efforts to make positive impacts on student achievement). In the first year of *Just Read, Lake!* evaluation, we observed a direct relationship between the active LLTs lead by the principal and literacy coach and the perception that the school's culture now focused on literacy. The culture has to change first, behaviors follow, and finally there are measurable differences in student achievement.

Beyond the LLT, the literacy coach has critical work: to develop professional relationships and include all faculty and staff in the literacy learning work. The LLT will communicate and represent the entire faculty, staff, and administration; but the successful literacy coach works with *every* member of the school's faculty, staff, and administration—not just selected ones. Above all, avoid any suggestion that the literacy coach has favorites or a clique that benefits from the position and resources. This negative perception could be fatal to the success of the literacy coach and improving student achievement. Those not on the LLT may need the most support, encouragement, and modeling to feel valued and important in the literacy learning process.

DISTRICT PARTNERS

As we have mentioned, all districts and schools should have an LLT. Many districts have a district literacy coach or a coordinator of literacy coaches. From the school-based literacy coach perspective, having a district representative on the LLT can help. The district representative should directly influence literacy policy and expenditures in the district. The school principal probably offers the greatest insight into what district level individual should be invited for this important advocacy opportunity. Often, this person has a title indicating a certain level of influence; but more often than not, the one with the greatest influence may not have the associated title. A district partner can guide district resources, may be an advocate in important circles of influence and funding, and may help provide direction and support that the literacy coach cannot anticipate. One word of caution: Request someone who will attend and participate in the LLT, not someone named for political reasons who may never attend. Literacy coaches need active partners, not placeholders, to improve the culture of literacy in a school.

STATE AND REGIONAL PARTNERS

Each state and regional service agency has support systems for designing, implementing, and monitoring literacy services prekindergarten through high school. Check out the Department of Education's Web site for literacy-related services. Contact Department of Education representatives and let them know what the literacy coach is doing. Invite support and participation. Unless the literacy coach is on their direct e-mailing and mailing lists, notices of opportunities for professional development, grants, or resources may not be received without making this contact.

Another opportunity may arise from making these contacts: the option to participate in funded research. Such opportunities can be advantageous. They can result in learning more about research-based literacy, making more useful contacts for the school or district, and providing opportunities to bring resources into the school at a cost-effective price.

HIGHER EDUCATION PARTNERS

The wise literacy coach contacts local institutions of higher education (both public and private) to apprise them of the school's literacy work and interests. Colleges and universities have and regularly apply for grants. If the literacy coach and school are the university's school partner in the grant applications, professional development, resources, monitoring support, and other opportunities may come the school's way. Colleges and universities typically need school partners to qualify for literacy-related grants.

SCENARIO

Rose Partnering on the Cutting Edge

A few years ago when working in a large, urban district as a district administrator, I lead a task force to develop a literacy intervention project for middle schools. The task force—now we would call it an LLT—designed the best classroom concept based on the available research. I reached out to a university researcher who had developed software intended for special education students reading below grade level. Coincidentally, the researcher was seeking an environment for piloting and evaluating the software. After some discussion, he was invited to demonstrate the software to the task force. Following the demonstration, the task force invited the researcher to pilot the software in the middle school literacy intervention project classrooms designed by the task force. The agreement was that the software would be provided at no cost to the district, and both professional development and monitoring evaluation of the impact or lack of impact would be provided by the researcher's grant. The literacy project was such a success that it was implemented in elementary, middle, and high school reading intervention classrooms. As a result of one phone call, this research project continued for three years and positively impacted the reading achievement of many students and the instructional practices of many teachers. Keep in mind that literacy coaches should reach out to potential partners.

PROFESSIONAL ORGANIZATIONS

Professional organizations are another source of information and opportunity for the literacy coach. These could be local, like the local unit of the International Reading Association (IRA) or the local Phi Delta Kappa chapter. Throughout our public school careers, we actively participated and held offices in these chapters. Through this experience, we influenced local mini-grants for teachers, scholarships, and professional development that was virtually free to participants. For example, the Orange County Reading Council has an annual conference with a $5.00 registration fee. The Phi Delta Kappa chapter has an annual research roundtable night. These kinds of professional organization relationships can support the work of the literacy coach and improvement of student achievement.

Besides the local chapters, the literacy coach should be active in state and national organizations. Through their publications, Web sites, professional development, and conferences, the literacy coach and other school and district professionals can continue to stay on the cutting edge of research-based practice and network with colleagues nationally.

SCENARIO

Partnering to Research

A large school district of about 60,000 students is concerned about the lack of literacy learning gains of their high school students. This dearth of learning gains affects the lowest performing students as well as those on grade level and in honors classes. With this concern in mind, the superintendent contacted a public university professor well-known for elementary literacy research.

Through that contact and ensuing discussion, a partnership was formed: High School Reading Intervention Research Project. This research project has just begun and will continue for three years. Although the district is committed to the resources of personnel, time, and instructional resources, the university is providing research-based intervention professional development and the research on the implementation and results. Publishers are working cooperatively with the district, so their literacy resources will be a part of this potentially important research project. Such collaboration and partnering with higher education is a win for everyone concerned: students, teachers, administrators, and the university.

TERMS TO REMEMBER

Literacy Leadership Team (LLT): This is a team made up of invited and volunteer representatives from the faculty, staff, and administration who work collaboratively to develop, implement, and monitor a school or district literacy system.

6 Monitoring and Communicating Data on Student Achievement

Ongoing assessment, a key component of effective reading intervention programs, provides important information about student abilities and the effectiveness of strategies and methods.

(Wilson & Protheroe, 2002, p. 79)

Data should drive instruction! The introductory quote emphasizes how important this is for literacy intervention, but it is important for all students. The emphasis on accountability has helped educators realize that data are necessary to ensure that instruction is effective and students are achieving. The literacy coach must help the school determine what data to use and how they are used to drive instruction. The literacy coach will need to determine the answer to several questions about data in the school: Is there a system needed for easy maintenance and access to the data? How can we be positive the students are making gains? And on which students should we be gathering data? What about data on teachers' students' growth?

The literacy coach and administrator will be well served to reflect on the many forms of data available, which other forms would be useful, and what data may say about effectiveness of instruction. In Chapter 3, we discussed the research-based literacy practices that the literacy coach and teaching faculty are encouraged to consider. Mentoring teachers to use the most recent research-based literacy strategies is the first step toward improving student achievement. However, besides consistently implementing research-based classroom instruction, monitoring student achievement data is the cornerstone to ensuring continuous student achievement improvement. This chapter will address the types of data, both formal and informal, that may help inform instruction; it also addresses how to use that data effectively with teachers, staff, administrators, and parents.

MANAGING DATA

Gathering data is the first step, and making sure that a system exists for storing the gathered data over time is the second step. Storing data from year to year allows the literacy coach to make yearly growth comparisons by individual students, class grades, and individual subgroups. Looking at data and comparing results from different school years is a good way to determine if growth is continuing or if the effectiveness of the current approach is leveling off or even declining. Ideally, the reader's school or district has a system for storing and comparing assessment results from year to year. If not, the literacy coach should have a personal data management system, such as a computer program. Printing graphs of results over the past three or four school years visually and effectively displays data, because graphs are usually easy for all stakeholders to understand.

Successful generals often have what they refer to as a *war room* or *strategy room* where they display evidence of their victories. Literacy coaches can use this concept to display graphs of data, newspaper articles related to test improvement, or student work. Find a place where many faculty members are apt to see the war room message: How we are improving student literacy achievement and what still needs work. Display data in as many ways as possible, showing school gains or lack thereof. These data are invaluable when the media representatives call or parents attend open house or visit the school. Remember: Only the principal or the principal's designee should ever speak to media representatives.

The literacy coach should ensure that school administrators, parents, and community members have this data at their fingertips. It is important to have data available that is easy to understand. For example, trying to describe a Lexile may be difficult, but growth on a standardized assessment may be easy to understand. Concise data simplifies the jobs of the literacy coaches, administrators, and teachers when it comes to discussing student progress with parents.

Schools and districts may be at different stages of gathering and analyzing data. Some districts have computer software in place that provides data for the teachers on their desktop computers. Other schools may receive hard copies or limited data. If your school or district is in the beginning stages of data analysis, Calhoun's *Using Data to Assess Your Reading Program* (2004) is a resource specifically dedicated to reading. Other resources that may help are: *Authentic Reading Assessment: Practices and Possibilities* (Valencia, Hiebert, & Afflerbach, 1993), *Succeeding With Standards* (Carr & Harris, 2001), *Results: The Key to Continuous School Improvement* (Schmoker, 1999), and *The Leaders Guide to Standards* (Reeves, 2002).

Literacy coaches may want to have a resource guide to help place and sort data through spreadsheets. It will help the literary coach to acquire the knowledge and skills to enter data, store data over time, sort data, and eventually the more advanced skills of including formulas in the spreadsheets. Another option may be for the school or district to have a data coach or school technology coordinator to assist with these data tasks. If not, the literacy coach should seek the assistance of the district technology coordinator. There are many forms of data available, from formal high-stakes state assessments to informal student observations conducted by teachers. Let us examine the high-stakes state assessments first.

HIGH-STAKES STATE ASSESSMENTS

Many states require students at various grades to take an assessment to determine student achievement, especially in mathematics and reading. Such assessments may also be referred to as *screening assessments* or *outcome assessments.* These results come to schools and districts in various forms, but the literacy coach usually will have to dig deep under the average (mean) and total scores to find the truly meaningful information. The literacy coach must disaggregate the data to determine how all subgroups are performing. *Disaggregation of data* refers to data study by subgroups determined by the researcher such as age, race, gender, grade, years in school, years retained, home language, second language classification, special education, poverty, performance, or combinations of the aforementioned subgroups. At a minimum, we recommend studying subgroups including gender, race, home language, years retained, special education, socioeconomic status, and performance quartiles. Additionally, the literacy coach will want to study data by achievement on subsections of the standardized assessments.

As an example, when our local schools look at their reading comprehension subsection performance, they find that the students generally do not do well on the strand of research and reference. This strand is composed of maps, charts, graphs, and other assessment items relating to locating and interpreting data or nonnarrative print, which is required by No Child Left Behind (NCLB) legislation. What courses and subjects naturally have these kinds of readings in their texts? Science, social studies, and mathematics. So, who should the literacy coach work with to improve reading comprehension performance on the subsection of research and reference?

If your state or district does not provide standardized assessment data in a disaggregated form, a working knowledge of computer spreadsheets is beneficial. Data in the spreadsheet may be downloaded directly from local, district, or state reports; often, however, the data must be recorded on the spreadsheet by hand. The more information the literacy coach can enter to the spreadsheet, the more valuable the spreadsheet. For example, if the literacy coach only enters student names, grade levels, race, and standardized assessment results, essential demographics such as gender and poverty have been overlooked. This is important because the greatest gap in literacy achievement historically has been between males and females; and white students generally have achieved higher than African American students, who generally have achieved higher than Hispanic students. The goal is to close these gaps.

Table 6.1 illustrates a basic spreadsheet that can be used for recording and storing data. Once the data has been entered, the literacy coach can sort by columns and determine data such as which students make up the bottom quartile or top quartile, whether the male or female subgroup scores higher, which race scores highest or lowest, or which subtests result in the lowest scores. Other data might be beneficial, such as recording if the student is served by special education teachers or is an English as a second language learner. Besides groups, identifying individual students needing reading intervention should result from data study. Using a spreadsheet such as this in landscape form allows for more columns for more data. The more usable data gathered the better, but do not turn literacy coaching into data gathering; save time to use it to improve instruction. Remember: The purpose of data study is to improve instruction for individual students and groups of students.

Disaggregated data offer the literacy coach and administrator a wealth of information that can be used to drive curriculum, instruction, and professional development decisions. Study the data in Table 6.1. Did both teachers show overall student achievement gains? Did all students show achievement gains? Are any subgroups performing lower than others? Notice Mr. Elchenko's class—specifically his student Williams, J. Would it be beneficial to know if this student received any further diagnostic screening or was in an intensive reading intervention? The literacy coach and administrator must know what gain in achievement score is considered a year's growth and what score is considered to be on grade level to make further decisions based on the data.

Table 6.1   Disaggregated Standardized Reading Assessment Data Example

Years: 2004 and 2005   Teacher: Mr. Elchenko

Student	M/F	Race B, W, H, O	Grade 2005	Subtest 1 2004	Subtest 1 2005	Subtest 2 2004	Subtest 2 2005
Cole, J.	M	W	10	320	346	298	311
Jones, W.	F	B	10	336	339	287	321
Smith, M.	F	W	10	342	362	288	322
Muirhead, P.	M	W	10	410	440	419	445
Williams, J.	F	W	10	229	215	236	235
Average				327.4	340.4	305.6	326.8
Growth					+13		+21.2

M = Male; F = Female; B = Black; W = White; O = Other; H = Hispanic.

Disaggregated Standardized Reading Assessment Data Example

Years: 2004 and 2005   Teacher: Mr. Delpit

Student	M/F	Race B, W, H, O	Grade 2005	Subtest 1 2004	Subtest 1 2005	Subtest 2 2004	Subtest 2 2005
Tolbert, K.	M	B	10	320	349	298	321
Clark, J.	M	B	10	306	332	267	321
Coole, T.	F	W	10	390	390	404	405
Hale, J.	F	O	10	226	256	246	286
Dillon, J.	M	H	10	299	321	306	359
Average				308.2	329.6	304.2	338.4
Growth					+21.2		+34.2

M = Male; F = Female; B = Black; W = White; O = Other; H = Hispanic.

The data may also reveal which teachers tend to have students with the highest achievement results. If this result occurs, take a closer look. Did the teacher who seems to have the students with the highest achievement scores also have the students with the highest growth scores, or were they high performing students to begin with? Maybe the quiet and unassuming teacher is producing exceptional student growth from year to year. Should the literacy coach learn what this teacher is doing differently to produce those results and possibly replicate the process for other teachers? Remember, while you are trying to build a collaborative and supportive relationship between the staff and literacy coach, data should be used to support teachers, not as a mechanism to identify poor teachers. That said, teachers who are not realizing literacy growth need assistance, and that is the literacy coach's work. It is the responsibility of leadership to intervene if there are performance issues with faculty or staff.

Schools often give annual additional assessments, such as norm referenced assessments. This particular assessment may not carry with it the pressure of the state assessment required for accountability, but the results may be useful. Maybe your school or district administers a subject area assessment or a locally created comprehensive assessment each year. Literacy coaches should find out what assessments are used in the district or school to help determine if the assessment will generate useful data. A similar spreadsheet used for the state assessment (Table 6.1) can be modified for other assessments.

Another simple way to help track students is to monitor their grades in other classes and their overall grade point average (GPA). Because literacy is the foundation needed to succeed in most content areas, GPA information can also be used to determine if the students are using their new literacy strategies and, as a result, succeeding in other content areas. Is there a relationship between GPAs or classroom performance and standardized assessment data?

The same concept of data study applies to end-of-course assessments that many schools and districts use. The nationally representative group attending the Literacy Leadership Institute identified end-of-course assessments as particularly useful.

DETERMINE ADDITIONAL AVAILABLE DATA OR INDICATORS

The literacy coach should look at indicators that are not assessment data. For example, has the school or district increased the time available for students to read by implementing accountable independent reading? Has the number of classroom libraries increased and, if so, in how many classes and by how many volumes? What about the school library circulation—has it increased or decreased? How has this impacted reading achievement?

The literacy coach, with the assistance of the school administration, will want to track student attendance. High absenteeism is an indicator that the students are not in school enough to learn initial reading skills or literacy strategies. Absenteeism is typical of below-grade-level readers, and it is particularly characteristic of older intensive intervention students.

Besides student attendance, the administrator may want to track teacher attendance. We find that the lowest performing schools not only have the highest student absenteeism but also the highest teacher absenteeism. If teachers are missing many days, either because of illness or possibly even to attend professional development activities, who is teaching the students? What are the implications for making decisions regarding this type of data? Some districts and principals limit the number of days classroom teachers may miss instruction, even for professional reasons.

The successful literacy coach is always concerned about the achievement of all students. Look at data targeted for the honor students as well as the large group of average performing students. What does the profile and membership of classes of gifted students look like? What steps can be taken at the earliest grades to address this data? Have Scholastic Aptitude Test (SAT) or American College Test (ACT) scores improved for the high school students? Has there been an increase or decrease in National Merit Scholars? How about the group in the middle? Has its assessment scores improved over time? Is the school retention rate and graduation rate increasing or decreasing?

High schools and middle schools often find that their highest performing students are not experiencing reading achievement growth. Many high schools are shocked when they study data on their honors classes to see the lack of growth in reading, even though the students are performing well academically. It is important to monitor the reading growth of *all* students.

Clearly, there is a lot of information to scrutinize. The more data the literacy coach can gather, store, and study from year to year, the more evidence there will be to determine the school literacy system's success. From there, the coach can take steps to improve it.

LITERACY ASSESSMENT SYSTEM

To create a literacy assessment system, the school or district should have assessments for several areas and purposes (Table 6.2). These are screening, progress monitoring, diagnostic, and outcome assessment. What is the purpose of each?

First, a screening assessment (often the end-of-year assessment for accountability) is necessary to provide the teacher or literacy coach with an overview of the student's current reading level and an indication of whether or not the student will need additional help to reach or maintain grade-level reading performance. Administering the screening assessment at the end of a school year allows time to place the students in the appropriate classroom for the following year based on the assessment results; it also may allow the student to be identified for a summer intensive intervention reading program. Whole school screenings are advantageous because they help ensure that any student in need of help is identified. For example, a student may be performing well as indicated by classroom grades but still need intensive reading intervention.

Table 6.2   Literacy Assessment System Example

Type of Assessment	Which Students Should Take the Assessment?	Purpose of the Assessment?	What to Do With the Results?	When?
Screening	Administer to students performing below grade level or to all students	Identify students who may be reading below grade level	Provide student appropriate reading intervention (tutoring, intensive class)	Administer at the beginning or end of the year to give schools more time to appropriately schedule students
Progress Monitoring	Give to students in reading classes or receiving intensive instruction identified by the screening or diagnostic assessment	Ensure that the student is making adequate progress or intervene	If progress is good, continue with what is working; if progress is not good, reevaluate and change teaching strategy	Periodically throughout the year (daily, weekly, etc.)
Diagnostic	Administer to students who are not making progress through regular instruction	Identify specific areas of weakness (phonemic awareness, phonics, fluency, vocabulary, or comprehension)	Design individual intensive instruction to target specific areas of weakness	As soon as it is determined that the student is not making adequate progress
Outcome	All students	Determine effectiveness of reading system and student growth	Consider supplemental or intensive programs to accelerate growth	Administer at the end of the school year, so results can be used for next year's literacy decisions

Second, progress monitoring assessments are used periodically during the year to track the student's reading progress. Typically, these assessments are given to students receiving intensive intervention reading instruction or students in an elementary reading class. The assessments may be used multiple times, making it beneficial to select a progress monitoring instrument that does not take long to administer.

An example of a progress monitoring assessment would be a quick fluency probe, which may take a minute or less to administer, and the teacher receives immediate results. The teacher and literacy coach will need assessments to monitor the student's progress closely so the teacher knows the student is improving and not falling further behind. If the school or district is using any type of computer-assisted instruction, such as *Scholastic Read 180*, the program comes with a progress monitoring assessment. In *Read 180*, the Scholastic Reading Inventory (SRI) gives access to assessment reports ranging from whole-class progress reports to individual progress and diagnostic reports. The value of these computer-assisted monitoring programs is that they usually compute growth for the user. The DIBELS (Dynamic Indicators of Basic Early Literacy Skills) is another tool that can be used for progress monitoring for students.

Student portfolios are also an excellent way for intervention or reading teachers to monitor literacy progress and keep a concrete record of student work. Portfolios provide a written record of student performance. Carefully choose examples of student work for the student portfolio. It is often valuable and motivational for the student to help select what will be kept in the individual file. Examples of items to keep in a portfolio are writing samples, end-of-text reading-accountability products, or monitoring assessment results. Since this portfolio is for the teacher to use, records of parent visits, conferences, and e-mails supporting literacy improvement may also be included—perhaps even notes on the student's participation in literacy learning out of school such as private tutoring or afterschool programs or reading experiences at the Boys and Girls Club.

Diagnostic assessments are the third type in the literacy assessment system. They are used to determine, or diagnose, which of the five reading elements (phonics, phonemic awareness, vocabulary, fluency, or comprehension) are weak and in need of intensive instruction. The diagnostic assessment may be given immediately after the screening indicates a problem or only after the child has received additional instruction and not improved.

Note that this is not an assessment given to every student in the school. Typically, this will be in an elementary reading or intensive reading intervention class. If the student does not respond to the initial additional intensive instruction, the diagnostic assessment should be used to determine what intensive instruction is required and whether the intensive instruction is required for phonics, phonemic awareness, vocabulary, fluency, or comprehension. Examples of these assessments are *Fox in a Box* (2000), *Diagnostic Assessment of Reading* (1992), *Comprehensive Reading Test* (2004), or the *Early Reading Diagnostic Assessment* (2005).

Outcome assessment, which may also be the screening assessment, is usually given at the end of the school year. It is often the one that all students take and may be the one your state uses to comply with assessment requirements of NCLB Act of 2001. These assessments help show student growth from year to year and may be used to determine the effectiveness of the school's literacy system. Some outcome assessments are used as an initial screening indicator for determining students who are in need of intensive reading instruction and possibly a diagnostic assessment follow-up. Although we do not recommend it, they may be used to compare schools, districts, or teacher and administrator performance by political entities.

READING AND INTENSIVE INTERVENTION CLASSROOM PERFORMANCE

Student performance in reading class and intensive reading intervention is another source of valuable achievement data. Teachers may keep records of mastery of content standards as well as overall course grades.

Table 6.3 is an example of a student reading log teachers use to track the types of books the student is reading as well as the time the student takes to read the book. The comment section is used for the student to write a short reflection about the book or recommend the book to another student. This is a book completion log and not a daily accountability log. This type of student reading log also helps incorporate the reading-writing process. Useful data gained with this type of log includes tracking the types of books being read as well as the amount of time the student is taking to complete the book. Notice that students are required to complete a book review and file it for other students to read. This helps other students select books that will be of interest to them based on the review of their peers. Some teachers do these reviews on 3×5 cards kept on file in a recipe box for student use.

Table 6.3   Student Reading Log Example

Student: _____	Grade: 4		Teacher: Moreland, J.
Book Title & Author	*Fiction/ Nonfiction*	*Reflection*	*Dates: Start/Finish*
26 Fairmont Ave Maclachlan, Patricia	Nonfiction	This reminded me of things that happened in my life. Book review is on file.	Start: 9/1 Finish: 11/13
Because of Winn Dixie DiCamillo, Kate	Fiction	The setting is like my town. My dog is my best friend, too.	Start: 11/15 Finish:

The literacy coach should work with the core reading teacher or intensive reading intervention teacher to help identify areas to be observed, such as fluency, and collaboratively develop an appropriate log to record teacher observations. Reading and intensive reading intervention teachers must listen to students read. Accountable independent reading time is an excellent opportunity for the teacher or literacy coach to conduct and record these observations.

Using the recording log, the teacher or literacy coach circulates and goes to the student. The teacher may ask the student to read aloud to hear fluency and inflection or ask the student to summarize the reading to check for comprehension. This observation may also be accomplished by calling students to the teacher's desk or area where other students will not be disturbed. Calling up five students a day for about a one- or two-minute observation will allow the teacher to easily observe a class of twenty in a week. This observation record will become a valuable progress monitor to determine if the students are progressing.

Table 6.4 is an example of a classroom log that could be used to collect more formal progress monitoring information. Some students may need regular monitoring in all areas; others may only need monitoring in specific areas determined by their diagnostic assessment results. The literacy coach can collaborate with the classroom teacher to develop specific rubrics for each of the five elements of reading. Table 6.4 illustrates how the literacy coach and teacher have determined the target scores for each area (in parenthesis); if the student scores below that target score, the literacy coach and intensive reading teacher will collaborate on appropriate strategies for student remediation. In the table, the student scored below the target scores in comprehension and vocabulary. Notice that because of the close relationship with comprehension and fluency, the student was tested again in fluency even though the first scores were above the target score.

Table 6.4   Individual Student Progress Monitoring Example

Student:_____ Teacher: Fontaine, Ed   Literacy Coach: Bogart, C   School Year: 04–05

Date	Phonemic Awareness (90)	Phonics (5.5)	Fluency (25)	Comprehension (800)	Vocabulary (5.5)	Comments
9/4/04	95	6	85	670	2.4	Comprehension & vocabulary intervention
10/1/04				700	3.0	continue
11/1/04			90	725	3.8	continue

Monitoring a student's reading level with an instrument that will provide the student with a range such as a Lexile score can help. The example given previously was SRI, which provides the Lexile. Books also have a Lexile range; the teacher can help the student select books for accountable independent reading and monitor that the book selections continue to move to higher Lexiles. This information will help the teacher and student choose appropriately leveled texts and determine growth. It is important for the teacher and literacy coach to remember that these scores are just a guide; a student can read on a higher level in an area of interest.

SCENARIO

Time and Data Management

The literacy coaches in Lake County maintain a log of their time spent doing different tasks. Their logs indicate that the literacy coaches spend a great deal of time, an average of 30%, with assessment and data study (Taylor & Moxley, 2004). At monthly literacy coach meetings, they discuss their concern about spending so much time in one area. They accepted their present positions to assist students and teachers and to make an immediate impact on student achievement whenever possible. Literacy coaches are eager for computer-assisted programs, either at the school or district level, designed to lessen their work time spent on assessment information and data study. This same scenario has been true every year the literacy coach model has been in place. Literacy coaches want to assist teachers with their instructional decisions based on data and be in the classrooms modeling scientific research-based literacy strategies. Lake County is in the process of completing a data management system that will help record and store data to enhance the time available for the literacy coaches to interact directly with faculty and staff on literacy instruction.

REFLECTION

Schools and districts should develop literacy assessment systems to make data management easy for all the stakeholders. The value of the data is to inform instruction, which is the target role of the literacy coach. Always focus on the overall goal: Improve reading, writing, and content learning.

TERMS TO REMEMBER

Disaggregate data: This refers to data study by subgroups determined by the researcher such as age, race, gender, grade, years in school, years retained, home language, second language classification, special education, poverty, performance, or combinations of the aforementioned subgroups.

Screening assessment: A measurement used to identify students who may be at risk or in need of additional instruction.

Diagnostic assessment: A measurement used as a follow-up to the initial screening, it helps determine which of the five areas of reading are in need of intensive instruction.

Progress monitoring: A monitor used periodically to examine student growth, it determines whether the student is making adequate progress.

Outcome assessment: A measurement used as a final assessment to determine growth, it is often used to determine the effectiveness or success of the reading program.

Portfolio: This is a collection of artifacts of student work, reading logs, and data on reading growth or lack thereof; it may also include parental contact information.

7 Supporting Intensive Intervention

I am embarrassed and ashamed that I thought these students could not learn to read if they arrived at middle school not reading. The problem was never them, it was always us.

(Coney, 1995)

Chapters 1 through 5 have identified knowledge, skills, and dispositions of a successful literacy coach. We have also provided helpful ideas for acquiring knowledge and resources for self-development. After building the schoolwide literacy team and the literacy leadership team (LLT), the literacy coach will have studied literacy achievement data on all the students (Chapter 6). While paying attention to literacy growth of all students, there is a population whose *teachers* may need immediate support. These students read below grade level, probably in the lowest quartile on a standardized reading comprehension assessment—your screening and outcome assessment. They may be second language learners or special education students or may have no identified need except they have not become on-grade-level readers. The services to be provided these students and teachers are beyond the core research-based literacy instruction and literacy infusion schoolwide. We call this literacy instruction *intensive reading intervention*.

WHAT IS INTENSIVE READING INTERVENTION?

Intensive reading intervention is when a student's reading performance is monitored and immediate intensive intervention must take place, beyond what is happening for the typical student in the classroom. Intensive intervention means more time, different instructional resources, smaller groups, and more intensity with literacy instruction appropriate to the student's identified lack of performance and developmental stage.

In the primary grades, intensive intervention may be for identified students who lack phonics and phonemic awareness, fail to acquire comprehension skills, or lack fluency (Snow, Burns, & Griffin, 1998). They have limited verbal skills or may be unable to write their names. Historically, many of these students participate in *pull out programs* in which they leave their regular classroom and go to another area of the school to work with a knowledgeable intervention teacher or assistant in small groups. This method may not have worked as well to close the gap, because the students miss the instruction on-grade-level readers receive while they are out of the regular classroom. More contemporary thinking suggests that the intensive reading intervention teachers join the heterogeneous (mixed ability) classroom and provide intensive support in the diagnosed area while students making adequate progress participate in literacy enrichment. Intensive reading intervention teachers in primary grades who have participated in both pull out and push in models reveal that their students are making greater progress with the push in model since their intervention work is more closely aligned with the regular classroom teacher's literacy instruction. Chandlers School in Logan County, Kentucky, implemented this intervention model for the 2004–2005 school year. At the end of the year, the school had moved from last place in K–3 reading achievement to first place within the district. Whichever approach to intervention your school uses, be sure it is research based; and monitor student literacy growth so instructional adjustments are immediate when necessary.

As students reach Grades 4 and up, the immediate intensive reading intervention may continue to take place in the classroom. More than likely, classes are content driven, and perhaps students even change classes for different content curriculum experiences. Not only may the organizational structure be different, complicating the issue of intervention, but the gap between on-grade-level readers or those making adequate progress and needing intervention is now much greater. Some schools will continue to have a reading class for every student in Grades 4 through 6 or even through Grade 8. We recommend continuing a reading class for all students appropriate to the developmental stage and literacy needs of the students up through Grade 8. If that is the case, support may occur within the reading class, just as it may for the students in earlier grades. However, students who read two or more years below grade level and are classified as having great needs in Grade 6 or above may need phonics instruction and practice. This may also need to be provided in authentic contexts and with developmentally appropriate materials and strategies for students who may not need phonemic awareness instruction.

In contrast to the intervention taking place in the classroom, most intervention for students in Grades 4 and up (particularly Grade 6 and up) will probably take place in another classroom. This is because there will be such a large gap between the on-grade-level readers and those needing intervention. Different elements of reading—phonics, phonemic awareness, vocabulary, fluency, and comprehension—will be addressed. Although rare in the intervention classroom—only about 5% of the time— phonics and phonemic awareness may be addressed throughout high school depending on the individual diagnosis of the students. However, students who read two or more years below grade level and whose grade classification is Grade 6 may need phonics instruction and practice but probably not phonemic awareness instruction.

The most important thing to keep in mind when intervening with older students is that besides addressing the elements of reading, motivation and joy associated with reading must be found. This lack of motivation, fueled by dearth of joy in the reading experience, exacerbates the gap; the less the student reads, the greater the gap. The respectfulness of the intervention can be addressed by the community of learners that reflects an academically and psychologically safe classroom. This classroom has high expectations of the students' growth and insists that mutual respect is afforded to both students and teachers. This respect will be observed in all interactions among students and teachers, the instructional resources, and the instructional experiences offered by the teacher.

INTENSIVE READING INTERVENTION CLASSROOM

For students who are in an intensive reading intervention classroom, at least 90 minutes per day (probably a block of time) of engaged literacy instruction is essential to close the gap or to make more than one year's gain in nine months of instruction. This 90-minute instructional time for literacy should include the nonnegotiable expectations of daily practice mentioned in Chapter 1. A typical intervention class period of 90 minutes for older students may look like the one in Table 7.1.

Table 7.1   Research-Based Intensive Reading Intervention Example

20 minutes	Shared reading (joy, phonemic awareness, vocabulary, fluency, comprehension)
20 minutes	Direct instruction about elements of reading and reading skills (main idea, point of view, summary, supporting details, paraphrase, etc.)
20 minutes	Accountable independent reading (vocabulary, fluency, comprehension)
20 minutes	Writing and reading relationship (comprehension strategies, graphic organizers, parts of speech, grammar in context, etc.)
10 minutes	Read aloud, class closure, put away materials, etc. (motivation and joy of reading, fluency, vocabulary, comprehension)

Of course this schedule can vary, but the most important concept is that all nonnegotiables take place daily. During the 20 minutes of direct instruction or writing and reading relationship, the students may cycle through literacy centers; the teacher may be one center, providing small-group time for targeted intervention. At the teacher center, students experience small-group interaction with the teacher and receive support in vocabulary, fluency, comprehension, writing, or whatever is needed. These students need consistent class organization and patterns of instruction to create an academically and psychologically safe environment. Consistency ensures that deficit literacy skills are instructed.

The example provided is not a template, it's just one possibility. Above all, the intervention experience, whether within the regular classroom or in another classroom, should be structured to engage students every minute of every day with research-based literacy learning.

Intervention teachers must not be mislead to believe that they need to entertain or coddle these students. A nonexample would be for the teacher to promise free time to students who complete their work. Free time is indulging and letting these below-grade-level readers have less engaged time. To close the gap in literacy, achievement-intensive reading intervention should be businesslike, on-task, and with every moment used in research-based learning.

We want students to believe that teachers feel confident about their abilities to improve in reading, writing, and content learning. Communicate confidence with high expectations and by investing engaged time. Persist in the pursuit of excellent work and celebrating that excellent work.

Expectations and Student Achievement

Rose's son, Jay, has described several experiences in school when he observed teachers with lower expectations of other students. As a young adult, he wonders what would have happened if all students were treated with the respect and expectations he was afforded.

In middle school, Jay argued with another student. As a result of their inappropriate behavior, the teacher asked each of them to write one page about what he did wrong and what he would do differently the next time the situation came up. When the papers were turned in, my son had written 1½ pages, since that is how long it took him to respond to the task. The other student wrote less than one page. At first, Jay was incensed at the perception that the other student did not have to do the complete assignment. Then, to make matters worse (in his mind), the teacher corrected his paper and asked him to rewrite it to correct the errors, sentence structure, and word choice. Yet, his cohort in the altercation neither had his paper corrected, nor had to rewrite it. When Jay complained to Mrs. Pat, she told him, "Jay, you are a good writer and you can be an even better one. I took the time to correct your paper, because I care about your success. You will really be someone important one day and I want you to have every assistance I can give you. The other student does not have your potential." In other words, in this teacher's judgment, Jay was worth the investment of time and high expectations, but the other student was not. Do you think other students knew this?

INTERVENTION ON NONSCHOOL TIME

Some schools intervene with tutoring, Saturday school, intensive intervention, reading camps, and other approaches that take place outside of the normal school day. Each may be implemented with funding obtained from grants or budgeted from the regular funds if the district allows.

Before pursuing interventions outside the school day, we encourage literacy coaches to verify that interventions during the school day are research based and working well. It is complicated to have a literacy system within the school day with intensive intervention with students and teachers consistently present, and it is more difficult to accomplish on nonschool time.

Having provided a word of caution, now let's proceed with some ideas. First, even outside the school day, intervention should be businesslike and research based, not entertainment, babysitting, or play. We have both observed afterschool or summer programs with great potential that result in students throwing footballs or playing games!

Here are eight questions to consider when developing a value added intervention:

1. Is the intervention aligned with the school day intervention?

2. How will attendance be required and monitored?

3. Who will be the teacher? Will the teacher be highly qualified?

4. How will the impact be measured and monitored?

5. How will it be funded?

6. How will the intervention be assessed?

7. Will transportation be provided for students?

8. Will parents be included?

In any grade level, if students are identified on the screening or outcome assessment as reading two or more years below grade level, a summer intervention between school years is a good idea. For consistency and alignment, the intervention for the fall term should begin in the summer intervention using the same research-based instructional approach and resources and the same highly qualified teacher. The importance of this consistency in expectations and organization grows as students mature and become less compliant. Seamless intensive intervention gives students a head start toward catching up and acclimating to a new instructional environment. Additionally, they experience a developing community of learners critical to creating staying power for the below-grade-level reader. This type of thoughtful approach to an intervention outside the normal school day will add value to the literacy system that is in place.

ASSISTING WITH MONITORING DATA

Intensive reading intervention students are fragile and are constantly engaged in research-based literacy learning. Since continuous monitoring of growth with commensurate instructional experiences is critical to improving reading, the intervention teachers usually welcome support from the literacy coach. Literacy coaches can assist in one of two ways.

They can give and evaluate the monitoring assessment, like Dynamic Indicators of Basic Early Literacy Skills (DIBELS) or Diagnostic Assessment of Reading (DAR). Or, they may provide literacy learning instruction to the students while teachers assess individuals. Either way, no learning time is lost.

Another support the literacy coach may offer the intensive reading intervention teacher is student observation and documentation. The literacy coach may work with the intensive teacher to identify areas to be observed, such as fluency, and help develop an appropriate log in which the teacher can record what is seen and heard. In the intensive intervention classroom, most students are not fluent readers, so teachers must listen to students read; it is recommended that they use a fluency assessment. Just as mentioned in Chapter 6, the literacy coach can assist the intervention teacher monitor assessment and make instructional decisions regarding the data the assessment yields.

Beyond required monitoring and diagnostic assessment support, teachers may need assistance with instructional interventions that emerge from lack of growth or identified needs. Once students not making progress or making less progress than acceptable are identified, how will a teacher know what to do? A successful literacy coach collaborates with the intervention teacher on instructional possibilities. Perhaps the literacy coach will model the instructional approach in the reading intervention classroom.

SCENARIO

Elementary Literacy Coach and Instructional Collaboration

Rose knows an elementary literacy coach who observed in a classroom for one day, then conferred with the teacher regarding possible options for instructional improvement. After collaboration, the teacher decided to create a listening center for fluency development. They worked together to create the center and even made the directions chart in print and pictures so the students could easily follow them. After modeling how to use the listening center for the students, the literacy coach helped them use the center and followed with guided practice. On the first day of listening center implementation, the literacy coach was in the classroom assisting each group of students as they independently rotated through the center. This type of support in the classroom with students ensures consistent,

INSTRUCTIONAL RESOURCES

Selecting instructional resources is always an important component of a successful classroom but never more so than in intensive intervention. In Chapter 4, we suggested that literacy coaches preview research-based texts and keep examination copies in their work areas. One of the literacy coach's most influential roles related to gains in student achievement is to be knowledgeable about intervention approaches and instructional resources for different students.

When the school is selecting an intervention model, the instructional resources should be research based and supported with validation research. Each time we receive examination copies of literacy resources, we note that the publisher is careful to include how the resources align with the research on acquisition of phonemic awareness, vocabulary, fluency, and comprehension. Generally, they also include validation studies in a variety of schools with diverse populations.

Once the instructional resources are selected, the intensive reading intervention teacher must have professional development on the implementation and use of the research-based resources. The literacy coach is advised to attend this professional development together with the intervention teacher to be in the best possible position to assist with implementation. Faithfulness to the validation model of the instructional materials is critical if the school expects to yield gains in reading achievement reported by the validation research. We are always surprised when schools purchase instructional materials validated on a daily 90-minute intensive intervention model and implement the intervention every other day. How much gain can they expect to yield? The expectation with half time is half gain! Although fidelity to the validation research of the instructional materials seems like common sense, please do not take it for granted.

The literacy coach should assist the intensive reading intervention teacher with implementation of the new instructional resources—from room arrangement and student movement to technology security and strategies for accessing or checking out accountable independent reading texts. Student achievement gains will be realized with increased student engagement for every moment allocated to intensive intervention. Keep in mind that it is unlikely that students in intensive intervention have had highly engaged literacy learning in the past; otherwise, they would not be experiencing such a discrepancy in their reading achievement. Not only will the intervention model be new to the teacher, but it will also be new to the students.

ENGAGING PARENTS AND COMMUNITY

Parent and community engagement is a way to add value to the excellent work of the intensive reading intervention teachers. Parents or caregivers of the struggling readers may not have had a good school experience and may not be good readers themselves. Teaching them what reading is and what they can do during nonschool time to support literacy development can add value to the in-school literacy experience.

> Parent and community involvement that is linked to student learning has a greater effect on achievement than general forms of involvement. To be effective, the form of involvement should be focused on improving achievement and be designed to engage families and students in developing specific knowledge and skills. (Henderson & Mapp, 2002, p. 38)

When we first think of parent and community engagement to improve literacy learning, we think of parent education. The literacy coach may plan parent literacy learning events with the LLT. Providing events at convenient times and places will encourage more people to attend. For example, the literacy coach may want to offer options for the parents to attend during the morning, afternoon, or evening. At each time, provide a snack and child care for younger siblings. As a middle school principal, this is how Rose enhanced parent and community engagement. The sessions may be at the school if it is located in close proximity to the target parents, or they could be held in a local library, church, or community center.

Instructional materials should be in both English and in the home language of the parent if it is not English. Print materials should be parent friendly and avoid educational language that will reduce parent or caregiver comprehension. When parents and caregivers attend the school literacy learning events, it is always a good idea for them to have literacy-related materials (books or magazines) that they can take home and keep. Budgeting for paperback books appropriate for the students' reading level and developmental stage can help create follow-through with the literacy learning that takes place.

Beyond the immediate parents and caregivers, there are other opportunities to engage community support for intensive reading intervention students. Consider the center of the students' community. Perhaps it is the church or the Boys and Girls Club. Maybe it is a community center. Within these community centers, there are influential people. Bring those influencers to the school or go to them and provide literacy learning. Teach them how they can support the target students. This may mean a computer lab in the community center or tutoring after school or on weekends. It may mean that these influencers apply for grants together with the school to provide additional support for students on nonschool time.

REFLECTION

The literacy coach who directly impacts student achievement will spend time supporting the intensive reading intervention teacher. When we monitored *Just Read, Lake!*, the literacy coaches reported spending about 3% of their time supporting intensive reading intervention at the elementary level. In contrast, the middle and high school literacy coaches reported spending about 14% (some as much as 20%) of their time supporting intensive intervention (Taylor & Moxley, 2004). This amounts to about 6 hours each week. Why do you think the middle and high school literacy coaches spent so much time with these teachers and students? Perhaps at the elementary levels, all teachers have reading backgrounds and teach reading. Literacy intervention is not new to elementary teachers, but they continue to learn how to be more effective. At the middle and high school levels, the amount of time spent with intensive reading intervention classrooms, teachers, and students is because of the lack of literacy experience of the teachers, the newness of the adolescent literacy research, and the challenging nature of the students. Literacy coaches should be prepared to actively engage with these teachers, students, parents, and classrooms K–12.

TERMS TO REMEMBER

Primary intensive intervention: Students who lack the reading growth in one of the five reading elements receive immediate intervention either in the regular classroom or in another area of the school.

Grades 4 and up intensive reading intervention: Students who read two or more years below grade level should be in intensive reading intervention classes or in differentiated instruction within their reading class. Although this may take place in the regular reading class, most often it is an identified classroom with unusual instructional resources and intensive use of more time than other students receive in reading.

8 Delivering Meaningful Professional Development

*Meaningful, intellectual, social, and emotional engagement with ideas,
materials, and colleagues both in and out of teaching are characteristics
of high quality professional development.*

(Little, 1993)

Throughout this text, professional development has been discussed because, in all possible forms, it may be the literacy coach's most important role and responsibility. To provide professional development, the literacy coach must become knowledgeable, internalize and own the knowledge, and be able to apply the knowledge at the work site. With this in mind, the successful literacy coach will know when to invite a consultant to provide professional development, when to investigate resources in higher education, when to call on a colleague in another school, when to use online services, and when to invite a classroom teacher or administrator to be the professional developer.

In this chapter, we discuss potential venues for the literacy coach's consideration. Not all venues will work in a particular setting, but always provide options. Professional development may be face-to-face or by way of technology, small or large groups, informal or formal, presentations or discussion. In Chapter 2, some options were mentioned. Here, we discuss specifics of meaningful professional development.

Have Transparencies Will Travel

A nonexample of someone trying to fill all the professional development roles is a colleague who makes transparencies or multimedia presentations like those from professional development she has attended. One of the least credible professional developers I have known regularly attends national conferences, takes notes, transforms the speakers' presentations into her own, and provides workshops. Not only is this plagiarism, but she lacks credibility.

The problem is that this professional developer has neither developed nor applied the concepts on her own. Although the literacy coach may not have applied all concepts in her own classroom, she can work with teachers to apply new concepts and strategies and share the results with other faculty. It's a good idea to partner the literary coach with teachers who are experts on different concepts and strategies. Together, they can provide these particular professional development opportunities.

PARAMETERS OF MEANINGFUL PROFESSIONAL DEVELOPMENT

Educators have experienced a lot of professional development, much of which was not meaningful. Effective literacy coaches will be sure to frame all their professional development with parameters that ensure success.

As Little (1993) suggested, high quality professional development is meaningful, intellectual, and social; it includes emotional engagement with ideas, materials, and colleagues. Teachers want their time appreciated; so when they participate, they want to learn something important with intellectual value. Professional development may focus on ideas such as fluency assessment or higher levels of thinking questions. Yet, the focus may be to ensure that teachers implement instructional materials as they were researched and designed or to understand the support available online or in the literacy coach's office. Little also suggested that teachers like the social environment and like to engage and discuss or have a voice in their own professional development. In other words, professional development is not *sit and get* but involves active engagement.

Also, whatever takes place in the literacy professional development should be immediately transferable to each participant's classroom or responsibilities. If professionals attend a literacy coach's session and do not find it engaging and transferable to their responsibilities, the number of participants will dwindle for the next session. Respecting one another's time and using it well is essential. We always ask in the beginning professional development, "What new literacy work have you been doing?" Conversely, when we are preparing to close, we always ask, "What ideas, concepts, or strategies have you been reminded of today that you will use in your class tomorrow?" Besides seeking a commitment to apply the concepts and strategies, these questions provide feedback and guidance to us as we continue to grow as professional developers.

ASSESSING PROFESSIONAL DEVELOPMENT NEEDS

Professional development does not just happen. It should be strategically selected, designed, and delivered. After careful data study on the strengths and weaknesses of student achievement, the literacy coach, principal, and literacy leadership team (LLT) should identify the titles, content, and delivery modes of professional development that are most likely to positively impact student literacy learning. Then the literacy coach can proceed toward meeting the identified needs in the manner selected by the LLT. Table 8.1 is an example of an elementary school's professional development plan.

Table 8.1   Sample Professional Development Plan

Date	Title	Participants	Resources	Budget
July 10–12	LLT Retreat	LLT	Notebook, articles, *The K–12 Literacy Leadership Fieldbook*	$300
Aug. 3	DIBELS	K–4	Handouts	None (District Pays)
Monthly	Essential Literacy Modules	Everyone	Notebook, handouts (handouts, resources in Literacy Folder on server)	$500
Biweekly	Study Group	K–3 volunteers	*Building the Reading Brain, PreK–3*	$300
Oct. 20	Motivating Reading	Everyone (nonstudent day)	University speaker Handout	$500

(Continued)

Table 8.1 (Continued)

Date	Title	Participants	Resources	Budget
May 1–2	IRA Conference	Principal Literacy Coach	None	$2000 (Reading First Grant)
Ongoing	Online Literacy Learning	Volunteers	Subscription to the Online Literacy Learning	None (provided by the state)

DIBELS = Dynamic Indicators of Basic Early Literacy Skills; IRA = International Reading Association; LLT = literacy leadership team.

Taylor, R., & Gunter, G. A. (2005). *The K–12 literacy leadership fieldbook*. Thousand Oaks, CA: Corwin.

Wolf, P., & Nevills, P. (2004). *Building the reading brain, PreK–3*. Thousand Oaks, CA: Corwin.

SCENARIO

Essential Core Professional Development Modules

In *Just Read, Lake!* (Lake County Schools, 2003), it was important to create a baseline of literacy knowledge for all faculty, staff, and administrators throughout the school district in elementary, middle, and high schools. Literacy coaches collaboratively selected the titles and outlined the content for each module. Following the collaborative work, pairs of literacy coaches developed the modules, presented them to their colleagues, received feedback, and then edited. The final product was a notebook and compact disk of *Nine Essential Core Professional Development Modules* to present across the district to every professional staff member. Although these particular modules may not apply in every school setting in every school district, the following list may help consider what would constitute essential baseline literacy learning for a given faculty, staff, and administration.

Just Read, Lake!

Essential Core Professional Development Modules

- Nonnegotiable Expectations of Daily Practice
- 5 Elements of Reading
- Accessing Text
- Reading To and With

- Accountable Independent Reading
- Literacy Strategies for Improving Reading Comprehension
- Vocabulary and Word Study
- Motivating Students
- Fluency (Lake County Schools, 2003)

For consistency in format and content, the literacy coaches agreed on parameters for each module. The nine parameters for the development of each module follow:

1. Note how each module relates to *Just Read, Lake!* (district literacy system).

2. Is research based.

3. Links to previous professional development.

4. Facilitates sharing literacy accomplishments and efforts between teachers.

5. Includes applications for each of the grades or curriculum areas represented.

6. Teaches, models, and practices the strategies, concepts, and resources within that professional development.

7. Is immediately transferable to the classroom.

8. Takes between 45 and 60 minutes.

9. Is delivered on planning periods, and before and after school. Make-ups are provided.

These parameters assure teachers that each module is part of a larger picture, not another new focus for the school. It ensures that their attendance will improve their own teaching. Teacher feedback is extremely positive, and instructional practices are changing in Lake County schools, particularly in the middle and high schools.

During the 2003–2004 school year, 95% of district teachers participated in all nine modules, which ensures a literacy knowledge baseline across the district (Taylor & Moxley, 2004). Although these modules provide a baseline of knowledge for faculty, staff, and administration, they are only part of the professional development offered to teachers.

It may be worthy to note that in May of 2004, the literacy coaches met and revised the initial modules based on their experience and new learning. They collaboratively created five additional modules to the list to be shared during the following year with faculty, staff, and administration. Ideally, this should be an ongoing process. Using feedback from the faculty and other participants, the coaches continually update the modules to keep them as up to date as possible. Too many modules create a delivery problem, so we recommend keeping the total number small and just revamping them yearly to include necessary professional development information. We originally created nine modules because there are traditionally 9 months in a school year; this allows one module per month to be presented to the school faculty.

WORKSHOPS

Workshops are a small part of professional development. As already suggested, workshops are a valuable part of the introduction and awareness of using materials, strategies, and concepts. Follow up with small groups, study groups, walkthroughs, modeling, and in-class coaching is essential if the literacy coach wants to move teachers from knowing to doing. The goal of professional development is to change instructional behavior, not just to know a few new things.

SMALL GROUPS VERSUS LARGE GROUPS

We have all been participants in large groups and know how easy it is to disengage. When providing professional development, seek opportunities to have small groups. The size impacts the quality of the discussion and engagement. Small groups allow teachers to ask questions, provide examples from their classrooms, and ask for specific applications. *Meaningful* is the adjective we want the literacy coach to think about while designing professional development. The goal is for the professional development to be meaningful enough to change instructional behavior.

The nine modules we have shared take place in small groups—during planning periods or before or after school. This is by design. A few literacy coaches at the middle and high school levels were insistent on delivering modules in large faculty groups. Initially, they met with far less success, so they have modified their mode of delivery to small groups when possible. Many of the elementary schools have small faculties, so professional development with the entire faculty works well in those cases.

WALKTHROUGHS

Walkthroughs are quick 5- to 10-minute visits in classrooms. Literacy coaches are not evaluators of teachers; the walkthrough is to provide feedback and coaching to teachers. Before a walkthrough, the literacy coach should provide baseline professional development to make the opportunity for literacy knowledge and expectations apparent. The purpose of the walkthrough should be made clear—to coach the expectations emphasized in professional development or requested by a teacher. Meet with the teachers, provide a copy of the checklist or instrument to be used, and be sure everyone understands it. Literacy coaches may use the Classroom Guide offered in Chapter 3.

When conducting a walkthrough, the literacy coach will only see a few of the items on the Classroom Guide. The coach should note strengths and areas to consider for improvement; meet with the teacher as soon as possible to share observations; and ask for clarifications, because the walkthrough only provided a brief window into an instructional sequence. The teacher should come away with a few good ideas or resources for scaffolding literacy learning.

MODELING

In the professional development sessions, the literacy coach should always teach, model, and practice with participants just as teachers should for students. The literacy coach must be the role model teacher. Always model the nonnegotiables in professional development, regardless of the topic of the professional development.

Do not expect teachers to try an idea they have only heard or read about. Following practice in professional development, the literacy coach should offer to go to teachers' classes and model the strategy or concept. The teacher hosting the literacy coach will observe and give feedback. It may be a good idea to invite any other interested teachers to observe and provide feedback to the literacy coach—perhaps using the Classroom Guide. The more the literacy coach takes these risks and invites feedback, modeling receiving feedback graciously, the more teachers will do the same. Here are the kinds of questions we may ask to invite feedback and model coaching:

What did I do to improve literacy learning that you liked?

What other ideas do you have for me?

Where did I stand or move during the instruction?

What types or levels of questions did I ask?

Who did I ask questions?

How did I handle incorrect responses?

What could I have done differently?

MENTORING

Mentoring can mean a variety of things. For the literacy coach, we recommend that mentoring be applied to every willing professional. This is a huge task; however, not every teacher will want mentoring.

At a minimum, the literacy coach may want to establish weekly sessions with teachers new to the school, follow up regularly, and mentor their literacy learning responsibilities. Notice, we did not specify *new teachers* but *teachers new to the school*. We encourage the literacy coach to use this opportunity to acculturate teachers new to the school into the culture of literacy and expectations of literacy learning. An experienced teacher has not necessarily learned how to be an expert in literacy learning. There are many practiced professionals who do continue to improve but repeat the same ineffective instructional behaviors year after year.

Literacy coach mentoring involves listening, offering coaching, assisting with assessment or understanding data, offering ideas, seeking resources for the teacher, and assisting the teacher to put a challenging experience in perspective. Mentoring means taking extra care to have a regular time to connect, follow up on past discussions, celebrate, and support as needed.

The literacy coach should help the teachers chart their growth in literacy, just as we might chart student growth, perhaps using the Classroom Guide as a reflection tool. The teacher ought to self-assess in August, November, February, and May. Now the literacy coach has a tool for discussing growth and continued needs, along with data for celebration. Sometimes when we do not formalize our learning, it is hard to recognize that it has taken place.

STUDY GROUPS

Today, study groups using quality, teacher-friendly texts are popular. They should be easily transferred to the classroom, teacher friendly, and developmentally appropriate to the students. High school teachers would not appreciate a study group using an elementary focused text; nor would teachers of primary students enjoy or be able to apply college-focused texts. Just as we select the right books for students, the literacy coach must do the same out of respect for the teachers.

Study groups should be organized and lead by the literacy coach. Some meet monthly, others biweekly. Each member of the study group has the same text and reads the targeted section of the text for each session. There are various ways for a study group to operate, and we suggest that each study group design its own rules. The literacy coach should be prepared to guide the first session. Then, perhaps each member or pairs of members will volunteer to lead a session. This makes each session truly collaborative, provides for the professional voice of each member, and encourages teacher leadership. At the end of the study group, celebrate! Participants may want to share something meaningful they learned and how the learning has impacted their classrooms. This kind of sharing (value added) motivates other teachers to sign up to participate in the next study group.

ACTION RESEARCH

Action research is another great way to grow professionally. With action research to improve student achievement in literacy, teachers will learn and document their learning and ensuing results. The literacy coach should be available to help these teachers create a plan and ensure that data are collected to document the success of the action research.

An example of action research is the science teacher who implements several new vocabulary strategies throughout the year to increase students' working knowledge of the new science vocabulary. The teacher may use a standardized assessment or end-of-course assessment, or compare current classroom grades to previous years' classroom grades to monitor the students' success.

The value of the action research projects is the teacher has tangible proof whether or not the implemented strategies increased student achievement. If using action research, the teacher should involve the school administrator from the beginning. The administrator will be happy to know that the teacher is committed to trying the new strategies and even more pleased to see the increased student achievement!

The reader may be wondering which students or teachers should be targeted for this type of action research and data acquisition. The students who are in the intensive reading classes are natural choices; because in most cases, efforts are made to raise their achievement level more than one grade level during the year. However, all teachers (particularly experienced ones) are good choices for action research because it helps them sustain their efforts to try new literacy strategies over time rather than give up if the strategy does not seem to work the first time.

STUDY OF STUDENT WORK

For student achievement to improve in reading, writing, and content learning, creating a community of learners among the teachers will help. The literacy coach can play an important role in accomplishing this collaborative culture. Invite teachers who teach the same course to have regular face-to-face time with the specific purpose of examining similar student work. This scheduled time is valuable: It affords the teachers time to look at student work and share new ideas for instruction, teaching methods, or materials designed to improve student achievement. They can determine what on-grade-level, above-grade-level, and below-grade-level work look like. The literacy coach may be surprised to learn that different teachers think excellence or lack of excellence is different work!

Teachers will benefit from observing the quality of literacy-related work produced in other grade levels and content areas. This scheduled time for collaboration will help infuse reading and writing across content areas. Little (1990) found that collaboration time can have the following improvements for both teachers and students:

Remarkable gains in achievement

Higher quality solutions to problems

Increased confidence among all school community members

Teachers' ability to support one another's strengths and to accommodate weaknesses

The ability to examine and test new ideas, methods, and materials

An expanded pool of ideas, materials, and methods (pp. 526–527)

Inviting teachers who teach the same grade level, like kindergarten or third grade or sixth grade, to meet together encourages collaboration across the grade level. Grade-level collaborations create consistency with the curriculum. They also enhance expertise with the common reading instructional resources and to resolve challenging issues of reading intervention. In these meetings, one third-grade teacher may offer to visit another's class to provide collegial coaching, while the literacy coach provides a literacy experience in the first teacher's third-grade classroom.

REFLECTION

Professional development is an essential role for literacy coaches in all grade levels. The target of the professional development may vary by grade level, but do not assume that teachers have the same literacy learning knowledge and skills as the literacy coach. We have learned that it is always better to begin at the beginning, develop a baseline of knowledge and skill, and invite participation in diverse literacy learning experiences.

Encourage the principal and other administrators to attend and engage with teachers during each professional development. Their advocacy, leadership, and follow-up with teachers are essential to create a culture of literacy and improve reading, writing, and content learning.

No one type of professional development will work for all teachers and administrators, nor for all literacy coaches. Keep in mind that adults, like students, need choice. Provide choice in the venue for literacy learning. If professional development is mandatory, offer a variety of participation times. Honoring faculty, staff, and administrators as they participate will encourage and motivate them to continue with their literacy learning. This is the only way instructional behavior will change to create a culture of reading, writing, and content learning kindergarten through twelfth grade.

TERMS TO REMEMBER

Action research: Faculty, staff, or administrators select a literacy issue and design a strategy to address the issue. Data are collected before, during, and after implementing the strategy. Learning takes place with this professional problem solving and research.

Mentoring: Mentoring involves developing a special professional relationship with a colleague to assist with knowledge and skill growth.

Study group: A group of colleagues or parents select a research-based contemporary literacy text to read and study together.

Study of student work: Colleagues gather regularly to study student work to create alignment of expectations, to offer suggestions, and to resolve issues related to student learning.

9 Managing Challenges

Many schools or districts have a set of values that solidly anchor daily activities with a deeper purpose. People know what is important. . . .

(Peterson & Deal, 2002, p. 13)

Throughout the first eight chapters, we have provided necessary background knowledge to effectively use the literacy coaching position in schools and districts. It is important for the literacy coach to establish a solid, collaborative, working relationship with the school administration, the instructional leaders of the school.

RELATIONSHIP WITH ADMINISTRATORS

Literacy must be foremost on administrators' minds, not displaced with the many other problems that face them today such as head lice, athletics, construction, and funding shortages. Literacy improvement must maintain an urgent status with the administrators and teacher leaders of the school. John Kotter (1996) referred to this sense of urgency as the number one requirement in his eight-stage process to successful change. "Establishing a sense of urgency is critical to gaining needed cooperation. With complacency high, transformations usually go nowhere because few people are even interested in working on the change problem" (p. 36).

The school administration must keep literacy a priority for this sense of urgency to remain high. To whom the literacy coach directly reports is important. In some schools, the literacy coach reports directly to the principal and in other schools to an assistant principal. If the literacy coach does not report to the principal, the assistant principal should be held in high regard by the principal and faculty to keep the literacy agenda moving forward. It is most important that regularly scheduled update sessions, probably weekly, are established to ensure ongoing communication.

The literacy coach should establish strong communication lines with the school's instructional leaders. For example, the principal could include something related to literacy on every faculty meeting agenda. We know of one principal and literacy coach who go the extra mile by modeling a literacy strategy at each faculty meeting to convey target information to the faculty. This is a great way to model comprehension or vocabulary strategies while ensuring that the faculty understands that important memo from the superintendent or content that faculty need to know. Try it! The results are amazing, and it is a great way to show the faculty and staff that literacy is important to the school administrators.

The literacy coach must always remember to involve the school administration. When the little victories are celebrated, the school administration should be the first to know. Many administrators have regular meetings with their assistant principals, guidance counselors, grade-level groups, budget committee, and departments. These administrative leadership teams are a great avenue for the literacy coach. The literacy coach should ask to be a regular member of these important leadership team meetings. Through these meetings, the literacy coach can learn what is happening, inform the school leaders what is going on with literacy, and be an advocate for literacy-related experiences. Remember, these are important meetings. Careful not to dominate, the literacy coach should take advantage of an opportunity to inform the instructional leaders about current events in literacy. Keep in mind the importance of the principal and assistant principals actively participating in the literacy leadership team meetings. They can effectively model the priority of literacy for faculty and staff.

We cannot stress enough how important the administrator and literacy coach relationship is. At the end of the first full year implementation of *Just Read, Lake!*, a survey was completed by the literacy coaches. One question asked, "What did the administration do to support implementation?" Here are two of the responses:

School 1: "Administrators attended all inservices, they conducted regular walkthroughs to seek evidence of implementation. Monetary support was great, if I asked for it I got it! Schedule considerations for low-performing students was given top priority—the administration was super!"

School 2: "They sometimes remembered to encourage teachers to attend the inservices." (Taylor & Moxley, 2004)

Which school has created the most sense of urgency and support for literacy?

CREATE A SYSTEM OF COMMUNICATION

The literacy coach must collaborate with the principal to establish a system of communication to report on the school's literacy progress. Chapter 6 illustrated several ways to gather and display data. Again, the first celebration should be with the administration. Next, the literacy coach should establish ways to report victories and other noteworthy literacy items beyond the school administration. If the school publishes a parent and community newsletter, the literacy coach may write a regular column to parents sharing ways the parents can help at home. This column can highlight literacy progress at the school, thus keeping the community informed.

SCENARIO

Literacy Coach Communication

One of our literacy coaches in Lake County, Pat Fisher, sends out a weekly literacy tip to all her teachers and staff. Pat also sends the tip to the district administrators and to other literacy coaches in the county for their use if they wish. Using e-mail to share tips like this has been effective. As a district-level administrator and university professor, we receive copies of the tips as well as Web sites and other literacy information that the eager literacy coaches have discovered. This collaboration is powerful and continues to foster the sense of urgency to improve student achievement through literacy coaching and the professional learning community.

TIME MANAGEMENT

Managing time may be one of the biggest obstacles the new literacy coach must overcome. Surveying more than 35 literacy coaches, we found that the data in Table 9.1 represents how they spend their time. There is variation among the levels served and among the coaches serving within levels. The percentages are means or averages of time spent in particular categories. Although we are not suggesting that this data shows how a literacy coach should spend time, we do believe the wise literacy coach should plan for these categories of time management. This text addressed each category from the research with the literacy coaches represented here and in other U.S. school districts. The time use shown in Table 9.1 is not ideal; it is a historical perspective of how other literacy coaches have spent their work time and may provide guidance for planning.

The data presented in Table 9.1 is worth close examination. As we have presented in previous chapters, it is of utmost importance that the literacy coach directly impact teachers and students. The table indicates that literacy coaches are spending almost one-third of their time on assessments and data management. Ideally, this percentage will decrease with the coming years as data are entered into computer systems for easier management. Attending workshops and meetings also consumes a large amount of time. As mentioned in Chapter 8, it is important for the coaches to become experts in the field; and with a shortage of certified reading teachers, literacy coach training is necessary. Ideally, where would you like to see the highest percentages of time spent? We would like to see a much larger mean percentage of time given to coaching core reading teachers, intensive intervention teachers, content teachers, and in-class modeling!

ACCEPTANCE BY THE FACULTY

Acceptance by the faculty will determine the coach's success. This acceptance, or lack thereof, may be a source of stress for the literacy coach. Note that a literacy coach is almost guaranteed that acceptance by all faculty members will not happen immediately! We have suggested that the literacy coach begin with faculty members who will work with them. Celebrate the victories that the individual teachers are making by working with the literacy coach, and little by little others will want to be associated with the success.

Going the extra mile to make sure the literacy coach is approachable and has an open-door atmosphere will encourage relationship building. Snacks, coffee, and drinks draw them in! Some literacy coaches provide tokens as reminders of the focus on literacy, such as key chains and pens with literacy reminders inscribed. A common literacy support and token is a 3×5 card printed with the nonnegotiable daily practice expectations.

Above all, the literacy coach should be a good listener. The coach must listen to the concerns or questions of the teachers, reflect, ask questions, listen some more, clarify, listen even more, and finally respond. Many times just being a good listener gains confidence. Some teachers will come in discouraged and want to unload; the literacy coach must be willing to listen and get through the negative before it is possible to refocus on the positive.

Table 9.1   Time Management for the Literacy Coach

Mean % of Work Time per Week Spent by Literacy Coaches

School Level	Number of Literacy Coaches	Providing Workshops	Attending Workshops or Meetings	Assessment or Data Management	Coaching Intensive Intervention Teachers	Coaching Content Teachers	Class Modeling	Meeting with Admin.	Other
Elem.	21	12.7	13.7	32.6	3.2	7.1	7.0	6.5	16.7
Middle	9	10.7	17.9	30.0	13.6	5.0	3.9	6.5	11.0
High	7	17.0	13.0	19.0	14.0	6.0	8.0	7.2	17.3
Mean		13.0	14.6	29.8	7.4	6.5	6.5	6.6	15.5

Taylor & Moxley (2004)

PERCEPTION BY FACULTY AND STAFF

It has been said that perception is reality. If this is true, how the literacy coaches are perceived by the faculty will be important. The coach may be working diligently on an important report using the office computer. This may be a valuable use of time, but the coach must get up and go to the classrooms. Otherwise, it might seem like all the coach does is write reports in the office. It is just as important for the literacy coach to be visible in classrooms as it is for the school administrators. Now here is a dilemma: If the coaches are always out in the classrooms modeling lessons and supporting the intensive reading intervention teachers, can they meet with other faculty members? Consider some sort of sign-in sheet or message board on which faculty members can communicate. Encourage the use of e-mail to set up appointments. Remember the idea of posting the calendar in Chapter 4?

PROCESS FOR ONGOING FEEDBACK AND DIRECTION

Continuous improvement is as important for the literacy coach as it is for teachers and administrators. Regularly invite feedback. The literacy coach may choose to use this invitation, Form 9.1, for feedback or may create a different system. Regular feedback means every 6 to 9 weeks, at least twice each year. If the literacy coach waits until the end of the year to invite feedback, it is too late to modify actions.

We also strongly suggest that the literacy coach use a system of feedback after each formal professional development. Feedback forms can help plan future professional development and meet the needs of the faculty. We recommend that the literacy coach have the participants plan for follow-up activities using the content of the professional development and use follow-up information to help schedule classroom visits and observe strategy implementation. These visitations can help motivate and assist faculty who may reluctantly come on board.

MONITORING OF EFFECTIVENESS RELATED TO TEACHER AND STUDENT LEARNING

Literacy coaches should prepare to make an annual report to the principal and leadership team summarizing specific accomplishments and their relationships to student achievement. For example, the report may identify numbers of workshops presented and number of participants, times

Form 9.1   Literacy Coach Feedback Example

Tell me how I'm doing
Name: _____   Date:_____

1. What literacy learning experiences have you participated in during the first nine weeks? (Examples: study group, in-class coaching, peer visits, class modeling, grade-level group, workshop, online, personal coaching, reading)

2. What literacy infusion have you tried?

    o How did it work?

    o What did you do to improve on the approach?

    o How did it impact student learning?

3. What am I doing as a literacy coach that is helpful to you?

4. What would you like me to do to improve my service to you as a literacy coach?

---

modeled in classrooms, sessions with study groups, and data study sessions with teachers. A clear statement of instructional change or lack of change on the part of teachers individually or in groups should follow. Groups may be by grade level, department, or study groups. This grouping depends on the literacy coach's work within the school year. The question is, "Did the literacy coach impact teacher effectiveness and student learning?"

SCENARIO

Race Horses, Turtles, and Rocks

The literacy coach is new to the job at a school that has not performed well for the past few years. The coach notices after a few meetings and interactions with the staff that the faculty falls into three categories. The first category is the race horses: Give them an idea and they are off and running. They are eager, often waiting at the door the next day to tell you all about how the strategy worked and asking for another.

The next category is the turtles: They will take an idea if it is spoon-fed to them, and they will try to get around to attempting it sometime when they have a free moment. The smart literacy coach knows they must work on this group, because just like the turtle and the hare race, they will hang in there and keep plugging along. Eventually, some of the turtles can even be transformed into race horses.

Finally, there are the rocks: This group needs dynamite to move forward. Sometimes, after the explosion, they land right back in the same place. The literacy coach knows not to use too much valuable time with this group.

Get the race horses going, they will run all day. Work with the turtles and help them plod along steadily. And in the beginning, avoid the rocks; they will come along later.

PUTTING IT ALL TOGETHER

We often ask literacy coaches, "What have you learned, and what do you wish you had known before assuming the position?" In this text, we have responded to the kinds of things literacy coaches say they have learned in their initial years: how to interact with faculty and knowledge about assessment and literacy. They also adamantly wish they had known how to organize their work and their time. This text has been developed based on our experiences with and observations of literacy coaches, both successful and less successful in a variety of settings. The checklist in Form 9.2 may be a good reflection tool for ensuring success for the beginning or experienced literacy coach and their supporters. Ideally, you are ready to implement successful literacy coaching in the school or district. The literacy coach position is a demanding and rewarding adventure!

Form 9.2   Literacy Coach Implementation Checklist

Task Accomplishment	Date	Comments
Knowledge of literacy appropriate to the students and teachers served		
Knowledge of teacher leadership		
Knowledge of coaching others		
Knowledge of certification required, and plan for achievement		
Personal professional development plan		
Office and professional development space		
Appropriate technology		
Budget/financial plan		
Professional resources for the literacy coach		
Professional resources for faculty, staff, and administration		
Student resources, examination copies, etc.		
LLT established		
LLT calendar developed		
Assessment system: screening, diagnostic, monitoring, outcome		
Disaggregated assessment data by student subgroups, teachers, assessment subsections		
Research-based intensive intervention implemented		
Plan for supporting intensive intervention		
Plan for parent/community engagement		
Professional development plan		
Relationship with principal and leadership team		
Time management plan		
Feedback plan from faculty, staff, and administration		

LLT = literacy leadership team.

References

Baumbach, D. (2004). *Making the grade: The state of school library media centers in the Sunshine State and how they contribute to student achievement.* Retrieved March 7, 2005, from www.sunlink.ucf.edu/makingthegrade

Beers, K. (2003). *When kids can't read: What teachers can do.* Portsmouth, NH: Heinemann.

Biancarosa, G., & Snow, C. (2004). *Reading next: A vision for action and research in middle and high school literacy.* New York: Carnegie Corporation.

Bluford series. (2004). West Berlin, NJ: Townsend Press.

Calhoun, E. (2004). *Using data to access your reading program.* Alexandria, VA: ASCD.

Carr, J. F., & Harris, D. C. (2001). *Succeeding with standards: Linking curriculum, assessment and action planning.* Alexandria, VA: ASCD.

Collins, J. (2001). *Good to great.* New York: Harper Business.

Comprehensive reading test. (2004). Lincoln, MA: Lexia Learning Systems.

Coney, F. (1995, June). Personal communication. Orlando, FL: Orange County Public Schools.

Costa, A. L., & Garmston, R. J. (2002). *Cognitive coaching.* Norwood, MA: Christopher-Gorton.

Daniels, H., & Zemelman, S. (2004). *Subjects matter.* Portsmouth, NH: Heinemann.

Diagnostic assessment of reading (DAR). (1992). Itasca, IL: Riverside.

DiCamillo, K. (2000). *Because of Winn Dixie.* Cambridge, MA: Candlewick Press.

Early reading diagnostic assessment. (2005). San Antonio, TX: Harcourt Assessment.

Fleischman, P. (1988). *Joyful noise: Poems for two voices.* New York: Harper Trophy.

Fox in a box. (2000). Monterey, CA: CTB McGraw Hill.

Gabriel, J. G. (2005). *How to thrive as a teacher leader.* Alexandria, VA: ASCD.

Harvey, S., & Goudvis, A. (2000). *Strategies that work.* York, ME: Stenhouse.

Henderson, A. T., & Mapp, K. L. (2002). *A new wave of evidence: The impact of school, family, and community connections on student achievement.* Austin, TX: National Center for Family & Community Connections with Schools Southwest Educational Development Laboratory.

International Reading Association. (2004a). Standards for Reading Professionals. Retrieved January 31, 2005, from www.reading.org/downloads/resources/545standards2003/index.html

International Reading Association (2004b). Coaches, controversy, consensus. Retrieved January 31, 2005, from www.reading.org/publications/reading-today/samples/RTY-0404-caches.html

Jackson, P. (1995). *Sacred hoops.* New York: Hyperion.

Kotter, J. P. (1996). *Leading change.* Boston: Harvard Business School Press.

Lake County Schools. (2003). *Just read, Lake!* Tavares, FL: Author.

Little, J. W. (1990, Summer). The persistence of privacy: Autonomy and initiative in teachers' professional relations. *Teachers College Record 91*(4), 509–536.

Little, J. W. (1993, Summer). Teachers professional development in a climate of educational reform. *Educational Evaluation and Policy Analysis, 15*(2), 129–152.

Lyons, C. A., & Pinnell, G. S. (2001). *Systems for change in literacy education.* Portsmouth, NH: Heinemann.

Marzano, R. J. (2003). *What works in schools.* Alexandria, VA: ASCD.

Marzano, R. J., Pickering, D. J., & Pollock, J. E. (2001). *Classroom instruction that works.* Alexandria, VA: ASCD.

National Institute of Child Health and Human Development. (2000). *Report of the National Reading Panel: Teaching children to read: An evidence-based assessment of the scientific research literature on reading and its implications for reading instruction.* Bethesda, MD: U.S. Department of Health and Human Services.

Nebhum, E. (Ed.). *Upfront.* New York: Scholastic.

Pavlik, R., & Ramsey, R. G. (2000). *Sourcebook.* Wilmington, MA: Great Source.

Peterson, K., & Deal, T. (2002). *The shaping school culture fieldbook.* San Francisco: Jossey-Bass.

Polacco, P. (2000). *Butterfly.* New York: Penguin.

Polacco, P. (1994). *Pink and say.* New York: Philomel Books.

Polacco, P. (1990). *Thunder cake.* New York: Philomel Books.

Polacco, P. (1988). *The keeping quilt.* New York: Aladdin Paperbacks.

Protheroe, N., Shellard, E., & Turner, J. (2004). *What we know about: Helping struggling learners in the elementary and middle grades.* Arlington, VA: Educational Research Service.

Reeves, D. (2002). *The leaders guide to standards.* San Francisco: Jossey-Bass.

Robb, L. (2002). *Reader's handbook.* Wilmington, MA: Great Source.

Scope Magazine. New York: Scholastic.

Schmoker, M. (1999). *Results: The key to continuous school improvement.* Alexandria, VA: ASCD.

Snow, C. E., Burns, M. S., & Griffin, P. (Eds.). (1998). *Preventing reading difficulties in young children.* Washington, DC: National Research Council.

Sturtevant, E. G. (2003). The literacy coach: A key to improving teaching and learning in secondary schools. Washington, DC: Alliance for Excellent Education. Also available at: www.all4ed.org/publications/literacycoach

Taylor, R. (2004, October 14). *Literacy leadership institute.* Unpublished notes. Dallas, TX: ASCD.

Taylor, R., & Collins, V. D. (2003). *Literacy leadership for grades 5–12.* Alexandria, VA: ASCD.

Taylor, R., & Gunter, G. A. (2005). *The K–12 literacy leadership fieldbook.* Thousand Oaks, CA: Corwin.

Taylor, R., & Moxley, D. (2004). *Just read, Lake! first year status report.* Unpublished report. Orlando, FL.

Time for Kids. MA: Houghton Mifflin.

Tovani, C. (2000). *I read it, but I don't get it.* Portland, ME: Stenhouse.

Valencia, S. W., Hiebert, E. H., & Afflerbach, P. P. (1993, December). Authentic reading assessment: Practices and possibilities. Newark, DE: International Reading Association.

Williams, R. D., & Taylor, R. T. (2003). *Leading with character to improve student achievement.* Chapel Hill, NC: Character Development.

Wilson, E. A. (2004). *Reading at the middle and high school levels: Building active readers across the curriculum* (3rd ed.). Arlington, VA: Educational Research Service.

Wilson, E. A., & Protheroe, N. (2002). *Effective early reading instruction.* Arlington, VA: Educational Research Service.

Wolf, P., & Nevills, P. (2004). *Building the reading brain, PreK–3.* Thousand Oaks, CA: Corwin.

Other Resources

Adams, J. J. (1990). *Beginning to read: Thinking and learning about print.* Cambridge, MA: MIT Press.

Allen, J. (2004). *Tools for teaching content literacy.* Portland, ME: Stenhouse.

Allen, J. (2000). *Yellow brick roads: Shared and guided paths to independent reading 4–12.* Portland, ME: Stenhouse.

Allen, J. (1999). *Words, words, words.* Portland, ME: Stenhouse.

Allen, J. (1995) *It's never too late: Leading adolescents to lifelong literacy.* Portsmouth, NH: Heinemann.

Allen, J., & Gonzalez, K. (1998). *There's room for me here.* Portland, ME: Stenhouse.

Allington, R., & Cunningham, P. (1996). *Schools that work: Where all children read and write.* Addison-Wesley Educational.

Allington, R. (Ed.) (1998). *Teaching struggling readers.* Newark, DE: International Reading Association.

Barton, M. L., & Heidman, C. (2002). *Teaching reading in mathematics* (2nd ed.) Aurora, CO: McREL.

Barton, M. L., & Jordan, D. L. (2001). *Teaching reading in science.* Aurora, CO: McREL.

Beers, K., & Samuels, B. (1998). *Into focus: Understanding and creating middle school readers.* Norwood, MA: Christopher-Gordon.

Billmeyer, R., & Barton, M. L. (1998). *Teaching reading in the content areas: If not me, then who?* Aurora, CO: McREL.

Blevins, W. (1997). *Phonemic awareness activities for early readers.* New York: Scholastic.

Burns, M. S., & Griffin, P. (1999). *Starting out right: A guide to promoting children's reading success.* Washington, DC: National Academy Press.

Calkins, L. (1994). *The art of teaching writing.* Portsmouth, NH: Heinemann.

Cisneros, S. (1984). *The house on Mango Street.* New York: Vintage Books.

Dynamic indicators of basic early literacy skills (DIBELS). Retrieved April 1, 2005, from dibels.uoregon.edu.

Fleischman, P. (1997). *Seedfolks.* New York: Harper Trophy.

Langer, J. A. (2000). *Achieving high quality reading and writing in an urban middle school: The case of Gail Slatko.* The National Center for English Language Learning & Achievement.

Logan, D., & King, J. (2004). *The coaching revolution: How visionary managers are using coaching to empower people and unlock their full potential.* Avon, MA: Adams Media.

Patton, S., & Holmes, M. (1990). *The keys to literacy.* Washington, DC: Council for Basic Education.

Rasinki, T. V. (2003). *The fluent reader: Oral reading strategies for building word recognition, fluency, and comprehension.* New York: Scholastic.

Reading Matrix. (2004). Retrieved October 7, 2005, from www.ncte.org/library/files/About_NCTE/Overview/ReadingMatrixFinal.pdf

Recorded Books, LLC. Prince Frederick, MD. Available at www.recordedbooks .com

Riggs, E. G., & Gil-Garcia, A. (2002). *Helping struggling readers at the elementary and secondary school levels.* Arlington, VA: Educational Research Service.

Robb, L. (2000). *Teaching reading in middle school.* New York: Scholastic.

Spring board. (2004). Princeton, NJ: College Board.

Stephens, E. C., & Brown, J. E. (2000). A *handbook of content literacy strategies: 75 practical reading and writing ideas.* Norwood, MA: Christopher-Gorton.

Taylor, R., Jones, P., & Mills, J. (2005, February). Literacy learning at Sebastian River High School. *Principal Leadership, 5*(6), 33–36.

Taylor, R. (2004, September). Literacy leaders: Improving achievement for all students. *Middle School Journal, 36*(1), 26–31. NMSA.

Taylor, R. (2002, September). Creating a system that gets results for the older, reluctant reader. *Phi Delta Kappan, 84*(1), 85–88.

Taylor, R. (2001, October) Steps to literacy. *Principal Leadership, 2*(2), 33–38.

Taylor, R. (2001, Fall). Teacher's challenge. *Journal of Staff Development, 22*(4), 56–59.

Taylor, R. (1999, December). Missing pieces: Aligned curriculum, instruction, and assessment. *Schools in the Middle, 9*(4), 14–16.

Taylor, R., Hasselbring, T. S., & Williams, R. D. (2001, October). Reading, writing and misbehavior. *Principal Leadership.* Reston, VA: NASSP.

Taylor, R. T., & McAtee, R. (2003, March). Turning a new page to life and literacy. *Journal of Adolescent and Adult Literacy,* 46:6, 478–480.

Taylor, R., & Peterson, D. S. (2003, Winter). RISE: Service and learning combine. *Kappa Delta Pi Record, 39*(2) 70–73.

Wilhelm, J. D. (2001). *Strategic reading guiding students to lifelong literacy grades 6–12.* Portsmouth, NH: Boynton/Cook.

Zutell, J., & Rasinski, T. (1991). Training teachers to attend to their students' oral reading fluency. *Theory Into Practice, 30,* 211–217.

Index